DANCE AND DANCERS' INJURIES

DANCE AND DANCERS' INJURIES

Chris Caldwell

CORPUS PUBLISHING

© Corpus Publishing Limited 2001

First published in collaboration with
The Northern Institute of Massage in 2001 by
Corpus Publishing Limited
9 Roman Way, Fishbourne, Chichester, PO19 3QN

Disclaimer

This publication is intended as an informational guide. The techniques described are a supplement and not a substitute for professional tuition. Whilst the information herein is supplied in good faith, no responsibility is taken by either the publisher or the author for any damage, injury or loss, however caused, which may arise from the use of the information provided.

British Library Cataloguing in Publication Data
A CIP record for this book is available from the British Library
ISBN 1 903333 03 2

Acknowledgements
Thanks to Lesley Ashworth for typing the original manuscript, the two models, Olwyn Maurer and Sean Pennington, to the staff and students at Merseyside Dance and Drama Centre and to my family for all their support. Thanks also to Manchester City Football Club for providing the inspiration to keep going.

Text Design Tracey Shooter
Cover Design Sara Howell
Main Cover Photograph Leslie E. Spatt
Photography Keith Allison
Anatomical Drawings Amanda Williams

Printed and bound in Great Britain by Bell & Bain Ltd., Glasgow
Distributed throughout the world by Human Kinetics – www.humankinetics.com – or:

USA
P O Box 5076, Champaign, IL 61825-5076, T: 1-800-747-4457, F: 217-351-1549

Canada
475 Devonshire Road, Unit 100, Windsor, ON N8Y 2L5, T: 1-800-465-7301, F: 519-971-9797

Australia
P O Box 80, Torrens Park, S. Australia 5062, T: (08) 8277-1555, F: (08) 8277-1566

UK and Europe
Units C2-C3 Wira Business Park, West Park Ring Road, Leeds, LS16 6EB, UK
T: +44 (0) 113 278 1708. F: +44 (0) 113 278 1709

New Zealand
P O Box 105-231, Auckland Central, T: (09) 523-3462, F: (09) 523-5462

Contents

Introduction

The following book is the result of seven years experience of remedial massage and three years as a resident massage therapist at the Merseyside Dance and Drama Centre. The college has a tradition of massage therapists over the last twenty years. These include Paul Blakey, the author of several books, including the best selling *'Muscle Book'* and Gordon Loughlin.

Indeed it was Gordon Loughlin who contacted the Northern Institute of Massage nearly four years ago looking for someone to replace him. Such was the quality of his and Paul Blakey's work, that the college principal specifically asked for a Northern Institute trained therapist.

As a tutor at the Northern Institute, I was immediately interested, mainly as I saw it as a new challenge and could apply my knowledge and experience in what was then relatively un-chartered waters, from my point of view.

For the last three years, I have combined my role at Liverpool with my role at the Northern Institute in Bury, Lancashire and various other posts. These have included massage tutor at the McTimoney Chiropractic College in Oxford, and locum therapist for Jim McGregor, a much respected physiotherapist on St. John's Street in Manchester, who built his reputation at a string of top football clubs. This is all cemented by the work done in private practice.

Most of the information and points raised in the following chapters come from my experience at Liverpool. I feel it is important therefore that the reader has an idea of how my work as massage therapist fits within the structure of the dancers' life.

Generally, the college provides aspiring dancers with a three-year full-time course. Most of the dancers are in their late teens. The year is split into three terms with similar breaks as 'normal' colleges. Most of the day is taken up with practical classes in all types of dance, including tap, ballet, modern and national. Additionally, there are classes in dance history and anatomy.

I work with the dancers once a week, usually Wednesday. They are all seen individually and make their appointments throughout the week with the college secretary. The principal of the college believes we are generally the exception rather than the rule in having a resident therapist, rather than sending the dancers out to a private practice.

As this book will aim to illustrate, many patterns emerge with injuries and their treatment and subsequent rehabilitation. Other issues highlighted in the following chapters include warming up and down and the use of pre-, inter- and post-event massage.

No sports person likes spending time out of their chosen activity, and dancers are no exception. Any given percentage of a therapist's time with injuries can possibly be avoided. There is nothing worse for a dancer, a teacher or a therapist than an injury that is either avoidable in its inception or in the length of its rehabilitation. This area will be discussed in Chapter 3.

After taking a closer look at specific dance injuries, Chapters 6 and 7 will discuss issues I have found to be important when working specifically in a dance environment, looking at an injured dancer, rather than just an injury. Also before drawing the book to a conclusion, we can all dream; we will have a look at ideal medical provision and how it can or should help the modern day dancer.

Therefore the following chapters are aimed at therapists, dance teachers and parents as well as dancers themselves. Whilst I am the first to acknowledge that until three and a half years ago I had no working knowledge of dancers, my knowledge of injuries and rehabilitation has been fully harnessed into a dancing environment through the work at Liverpool.

Chapter 1
An Overview

When one sees an injury, whether to a dancer or another sports person, the first part of any treatment, particularly the initial treatment should always involve a detailed analysis of the process or factors that have caused the injury. Any therapist will agree that this is an acquired skill in itself; it is neither an interview with a clipboard or an informal ten minutes of 'chit-chat'. After several years in practice, it has become somewhat easier than it was in those first heady weeks. The therapist has to remember the ideas that the client will be nervous and in pain, possibly afraid of the treatment, or worried about a possible career-threatening injury. This can prey upon the mind of the client to such an extent that information given during this 'history taking' session is sometimes hazy and inaccurate. However, ones favourite attitude to history taking and initial consultations is the *Kevin and Perry Syndrome*, the characters portrayed on the *Harry Enfield Show* (BBCTV), whereby injured teenagers sit awkwardly between parents and proceed to give no information whatsoever about the injury! If it is any consolation to young female dancers, this usually applies to the lads!

Therefore, as one can see, there are problems that arise even before treatment begins. However, if the history taking is done properly, it can give you a head start in the rehabilitation of an injury. I have found with dancers (and most injuries) that the first factors to find out are if the injury is chronic or acute, and if it was caused by overuse or impact. Firstly, with chronic and acute, this is ascertaining when the injury took place. An acute injury is one that has happened very recently, within the previous 48–72 hours. In most cases. Anything after that period of time can start to be classified as chronic. I once asked a lady in 1995 how long she had had the back pain she was suffering. After a short pause, during which time I was anticipating an answer along the lines of 6 weeks to 6 months came the reply since 1947. Definitely a chronic injury!

The other choice to make at this stage, is whether the injury is due to impact or overuse. Both these are reasonably straightforward. An impact injury can usually be described as a one off event or fall usually leading to some sort of sprain, strain, dislocation or break. Going over on an ankle when landing from a jump is a particularly common impact injury amongst dancers. An overuse injury is one that evolves over a period of hours, days, weeks, months or even years.

Dancers and non dancers alike have all 'overdone' it at some stage, whether decorating, gardening, training in the gym or in the case of a dancer, literally dancing too often and too long, causing either a multitude of aches and pains or something more specific. If ever a dancer complains of pain or injury in two similar areas, e.g. two knees, two hips or two shoulders, it is in my experience, highly likely to be an overuse injury.

On the face of it, chronic, acute, impact and overuse seem like four pigeonholed areas. However, in practice they very much blur at the edges, if not becoming completely interchangeable. For example, Briggs (2000) talks of making a chronic injury into an acute one, by breaking down the adhesive tissue that hampers joint mobility and integrity. We can also ask if an impact injury is the cause of an old overuse injury, and indeed if an overuse injury is being caused by the protection of an impact injury.

All the above scenarios are practical examples that can happen in all walks of life, but I have found them to be particularly true of dancers. From my experience with dancers, and after studying my records I would suggest up to about 15% of injuries are impact led, leaving the vast majority as overuse injuries.

As a massage therapist to dancers I see one of my roles as preventing injuries in the first place, usually through advice and education. To improve my own knowledge I observe dancers; not just dancing, but in their day to day lives around college. This has led me to linking dozens of ideas together about dancers and the causes of injuries; from studio temperature to diet and everything in between. These will be discussed in the remainder of this chapter.

The main thing these factors effecting injury have in common, rather frustratingly, is that they are in many cases avoidable. One area of injury treatment that is soon picked up on by the therapist is 'risk management' and its association to rehabilitation. Most sports people – and dancers are no exception – seem to believe that once they are away from the environment that caused the original injury, then its recovery ceases until they return. I have seen many an injured client doing something completely against their rehabilitation strategy, but because they are out of their dance environment they think it will have no negative repercussions on the injury and its recovery rate. I have seen many a dancer 'stomping' round shopping centres or in pubs and clubs with stilettos on whilst nursing calf or Achilles problems! As with any sport, people take their bodies for granted. If your body is reliable and in good shape, what can go wrong – indeed!

The first area we can look at is equipment, and with that we can include facilities. Anybody with an interest in athletics will know that multi-event athletes have a kit bag that mirrors that, with different types of spikes and clothing. The same parallel can be used for dancers. As a therapist, you can tell by the dancers' outfit which genre of dance they have been practising. Within each area of dance comes a different outfit, such as tap shoes, ballet shoes, leotards, skirts or tights. All of these need to be specific for each dancer and each type of dance.

It amazes and horrifies the therapist in equal measure to see dancers swapping footwear with each other – real life Cinderella's – without the fairytale outcome in most cases! All types of clothing, footwear and props carry a real threat to existing injuries and old weaknesses and can cause new injuries. In an ideal world, all dancers would have several pairs of shoes for each discipline broken in at the same time. It seems that a lot of dancers wear one pair of shoes and use them until they fall apart. The cost of this in terms of injury surely outweighs the undoubted financial burden of buying new shoes. Once the shoes lose their support, firmness and cushioning, the risk of injury to the dancer intensifies greatly, usually causing niggling injuries that may originally be labelled as overuse injuries, or repetitive strain problems, when in reality they have been accentuated, if not originated, by worn out footwear. This, as has already been said is a chronic situation, although it can also cause acute problems if inappropriate footwear leads a dancer to land badly or fall.

Another area that is extremely important in relation to dance and injury is rest. This can be explained in several ways, such as; rest within the day to day timetable of dance; complete rest when injured; active rest; a break from activity for a long period and also rest that incorporates sleep. Daley Thompson, the former Olympic champion, once stated that the most important day of his training routine was his day of rest. This is when he could recuperate and reflect. The same is true of dancers. Rest, in all its guises is extremely important. This can be looked at both physiologically and psychologically. When the body is being pushed to its limit, as in dance, all the various systems of the body are working to create the exquisite movement and control delivered by dancers – it is only when the body is resting that it can recover. On a psychological level, it is important that a dancer's schedule is well organised with the issue of rest well addressed. If all a dancer can see in front of them is a treadmill of dance, dance and more dance it may cause a negative effect that can in turn lead to injury, through lack of concentration and fatigue.

Whilst rest is vitally important for both recovery and prevention, it should be controlled rest rather than necessitated rest. Rest has been shown to be advantageous. However, it can have a negative effect on a day to day basis from a physiological point of view. This will vary from dancer to dancer and college to college. In my experience, dance colleges embrace a typical college timetable. This means a fragmented day; 9am start, break time at 10.45am, lunch for an hour at 12.30pm and another break mid-afternoon

Most of the lesson time is in practical classes. However, it should be noted that most dancers do have academic studies in dance history and anatomy. Even within a practical class, there will be times when dancers are active and inactive, short or sustained bursts of activity followed by unspecified periods of 'rest', whilst listening to or watching a teacher or other students. It is in this phase of rest, that the body will change, heart rate will lower, lactic acid will gather leaving the body prone to injury, during a burst of activity similar to a sprinter. This is an observation of the reality for a dancer and not necessarily a criticism.

When a dancer comes to me with an injury, the conversation invariably leads to warming up. It seems in many cases that a limbering class or bar work first thing in the morning constitutes warming up for the entire duration of a day. This is not adequate and as soon as the dancer rests for any period of time, a new warm up should be undertaken. Yes, I know, not practical, no time, etc. Therefore, this enforced rest within a day can cause complications, and should not be seen as ideal.

The last chapter of this book will deal with ideal medical provision for dancers. Some colleges provide better than others. It may be that a dancer has access to an on site physiotherapist once a week. It is safe to say that for a lot of conditions, one of the most effective parts of the treatment is rest. However, we must at this stage be sure of what we mean by this truly four letter word.

One may tell a dancer with a sprained ankle to rest so as not to make the injury worse, and to aid the recovery. What we will probably mean here is rest from weight bearing, stressful exercise, and in a severe case, the possible use of crutches. What we will also mean by rest in this case is doing stretching and mobility work, where possible, to other body parts, e.g. hamstring, abdominal, neck and shoulders, etc. What we do not mean by rest is sitting with one's feet up, doing nothing that will help with recovery from injury.

Another type of rest is almost a contradictory term, i.e. 'active rest'. This phrase can be used possibly for a chronically injured dancer with some sort of overuse or repetitive strain injury. It may be that the dancer will be advised to rest from classes that are causing the injury, but to try and keep a level of fitness that will not aggravate the injury. They may be prescribed some form of alternative exercise, possibly swimming or another cardiovascular activity.

Finally, we shall mention a more traditional meaning for the term rest. I frequently discuss what my dancers will be doing during their various holidays at Christmas, Easter and Summer. I frequently get the same answer – sleeping! In my mind it conjures up an amusing picture of a period of hibernation. However, if one is to study this more closely it does have a far more serious angle to it. Firstly, it gives us the impression that the dancer has given that much over the previous months, all they want to do, in fact, all they can do, is rest. Terms such as injury, treatment and rehabilitation, may be considered here. One particular term to be addressed is injury management, i.e. managing an injury. A lot of the problems I see as a therapist are injuries that I have to manage. Dancers a lot of the time, simply want to know the severity of an injury, be patched up and get on with it. I find myself, rightly or wrongly, telling dancers that we can 'patch them up' or 'keep them going' but that the real recovery will not take place until they have a couple of weeks rest at Easter or in the Summer. One physiotherapy session a week on an active dancer will not be enough to completely eradicate some chronic injuries.

It should also be noted that inactive rest during holiday periods can cause problems when the dancer comes back raring to go for their new term, eager to impress, keen to learn – the perfect scenario for picking up an injury. This can be seen on a smaller scale on Mondays, when dancers seem more susceptible to injury than at any other time in the week, straight after two days of inactivity in a lot of cases.

Therefore, rest when used properly is vitally important to a dancer. However, if it is abused, consciously or not, it can and will lead to a complication of outstanding injuries and a contributory factor of new injuries.

It can help injury rehabilitation if dancers help themselves. At the end of the day, different injuries can take differing lengths of time to recover. However, there are many factors that can cause and effect injury. We have already talked about equipment and rest, but there are other variable factors that can contribute to both new and existing injuries.

Dancers must give themselves the best environment in which to exist whether they are injured or not. This can involve variables such as diet, home surroundings, living environment, non-dance lifestyle, etc. To look at a dancer in action, most people think of words such as grace, poise and elegance. However, to gain these attributes, two less glamorous words are required – strength and power. To gain all this, the dancer uses a lot of energy, burns a lot of calories, and so should eat well. This is not always the case. For differing reasons, one can be bad management – "I got up late and had no breakfast." In other cases it can be down to body image problems, and, "Am I the right shape to be a dancer?" "Do I need to lose weight?" and, "Do you think I have lost weight?" These are all questions and phrases that I hear on a regular basis.

Ideally a dancer should have a big breakfast, supplemented by healthy snacks during the day, followed by a typical evening meal. Use of multivitamins will also help, as will plenty of water, drunk in small amounts regularly. Dancers should assimilate plenty of carbohydrate and protein, but also a little fat from time to time will not hurt! It is the time and amount of food that is important. Skipping breakfast is helping (or fooling) no-one and can lead to fainting and dizziness, endangering the dancer and others in close proximity.

Over my years working with dancers, I have seen an interesting pattern emerging, which has been noticed and confirmed by dance teachers too. This is that dancers who live at home with their parents are less prone to injury than those who live in a student environment, in most cases nearer to their college. On further study of this phenomenon, there are several straightforward reasons for this. These include:

• Dietary implications;
• Financial implications;
• Peer group pressure;
• Rest/sleep implications;
• Home comforts, and;
• Parental support.

Many of the above are inter-connected.

The first point about diet is a simple one. Most dancers who take on a 'student identity' cannot cook or will not cook and stand a lot better chance of having a wholesome balanced diet by living at home.

Obviously financial implications are not black and white in terms of where a student lives, but it may be that living away from home, a dancer has too much financial management responsibility. If they were still at home, a lot of this burden of responsibility would be taken by the parents.

One area that will be addressed when the dance college environment is looked at is peer group pressure, but this can be important in a student accommodation environment. Are dancers pressurised into too much socialising if they are living together? The dancers who live at home talk of 'being glad to get away from it all' and of 'getting off the treadmill'. This idea can link into our already discussed area of rest and sleep. Having been a student in halls of residence and student houses, they are not the best places to get rest and sleep – not at night anyway – nor are they likely to have all the creature comforts of being at home. The main example here is access to a bath! Many dancers pride themselves on soaking in the bath, and it does seem to ease many an ache and strain. However, due to time and/or space, student accommodation is likely to mean showers only.

Finally in this area, living at home is likely to lead to more direct parental support and old fashioned TLC – many dancers and sports people require plenty of this. Therefore, many dancers who live away from home are unwittingly increasing their risk of picking up an injury!

Up to now in this chapter, we have discussed various factors that can cause and effect injuries without particularly looking at the environment, surroundings and culture of a dance studio and its inhabitants.

The focal point of the dance studio is usually the teacher. They are responsible for the safety of the dancers on every level. Is the size of the group applicable to the size of the studio? Have the dancers got their own space in which to work? Can the teacher see all the dancers at the same time? Can the dancers see the teacher at all times? In an ideal world, all the answers to these questions would be yes.

The main task of the teacher is to hone technique and fine-tune routines. If this wasn't enough, there are other things they should look for, such as dancers 'hiding' injuries, or dancers with bad technique that can cause injury. Are all the dancers wearing the right equipment? Has an adequate level of warming up been undertaken? Is the studio temperature at the right level? Is there unnecessary clutter in the studio that can cause obstacles?

The experienced teacher should be on top of all sorts of situations like this, particularly when an existing injury is the topic. It can be frustrating for the injured dancer who needs rest, although, it is equally frustrating when that dancer feels pressure to dance through an injury by their peers, or even more worryingly, by teachers.

At Merseyside Dance and Drama Centre, the system seems to work most of the time. The physiotherapist usually has the final say and would report to the Principal which dancers should rest, and which should mark. However, talking to other dance students, it does not appear that this is always the case. It must also be noted that some dancers carry on regardless of what advice they have been given!

When dancers are compared to other sports people, it can be noted that probably 95% of 'work' takes place in the dance studio, with too many goals to afford any specificity to training. It seems dancers have to 'peak' for twelve months of the year for exams, auditions, rehearsals and shows. This differs to other sports such as athletics, rugby, football and swimming, where performers have several different aspects to training, depending on the time of year and all have defined seasons. All the above sports spend less time at their specific sport than dancers and more time on physical conditioning. This is not a criticism of dance but more an acknowledgement of the many facets of dance that need hours of practise to perfect.

To summarise this chapter, it can be said that there are many factors affecting injury and its rehabilitation. It is the responsibility of everyone involved with dancers: teachers, parents, physiotherapists and not least dancers themselves, to minimise the variable factors that can cause new injuries and prolong existing ones.

Chapter 2
The Use of Massage and Pre-, Inter- and Post-event Massage

Dancers may be viewed as the equal of athletes in terms of physical activity. Vincent (1999) referred to research that evaluated sixty-one different athletic activities according to physical, mental and environmental demands; ballet ranked second only to football by the selected criteria. Dancers twist and turn, leap and stride, run and dive. In short, they make and use all the movements involved in athletic or sporting events. They use all the major systems of the body and all the major articulations as vigorously and as skillfully as sprinters, high jumpers, tennis players, boxers and all the other sports people at all levels.

Dancers are susceptible to the same variety of injuries as sports people. Dance often places extreme and unusual demands upon the body (Arnheim, 1999). They strain muscles, sprain joints, sustain traumatic impact injuries and suffer from a range of overuse syndromes. I have treated many dancers suffering from hamstring strains, chronic inflammation of the Achilles tendon, 'shin splints' and low back pain. Dancers, on occasions, collide with their environment. One dancer may leap right into the path of another dancer just as two soccer players may accidentally collide when, eyes steadily on the ball, they run into each other. A dancer may accidentally fall off a stage or bump into scenery just as a cyclist may fall from his bike or a rugby player run into a goal post.

Most athletes nowadays have a good understanding of the value of a warm up prior to participation in training or an event. It is not unusual to see soccer players out on the pitch thirty minutes before kick-off time going through a part of their warm up routine. Some soccer clubs include massage in the warm up schedule. A sprinter will take anything between forty minutes and an hour, following his or her procedures for warming up prior to competition. Many sprinters, indeed many athletes, include some form of massage in their immediate preparations for competition or a hard training session.

Massage is not just a matter of a comforting 'rub down' afterwards. Massage can be used in different ways to suit the individual and to suit the circumstances. Many think of massage as a way of soothing or easing the body after vigorous physical activity; others may think of massage in a more remedial way of treating an injury. Many athletes and sports people endeavour to have a massage treatment after a game of football, an afternoon of tennis or a long run. Others bring their remedial massage therapist to help treat a sprained ankle or low back pain. This is fine. Massage is very effective and useful in the post-event or injury situation.

Massage also has a valuable part to play in the pre-activity phase, i.e. before the game, race, training session, or dance session. Let us examine how massage can be adapted for the benefit of dancers not only in the pre-dance and the post-dance situation but also in between sessions on the same day.

The History of Pre-activity Massage

Sports people (and probably dancers) have always received some form or other of massage to help them prepare and recover from their sporting activities. There are documentary accounts of the application of massage for the benefit of athletes from both ancient Greece and Rome. Galen served his medical apprenticeship tending the injury needs of the gladiators. These origins of sports massage are mostly clouded by the mists of time but surely the ancient practitioners must have developed their special techniques for pre-event massage, restorative massage and remedial massage. It would be fascinating to have a really good, eye-witness account.........

In more recent times, sports massage has developed and become very popular. Hungerford (1993) regarded 1972 as the key date in the development of modern sports massage. She claimed that the resurgence of sports massage was the result of the success of Lasse Viren in the Olympic Games. This Finnish athlete won the gold medals in both the 5,000m and 10,000m; an almost impossible feat at the same Olympics. The principal difference between Viren and other, less successful runners, was that he received massage treatment on a daily basis both to prepare for his training and racing and as a restorative treatment. What was good enough for Lasse Viren........

In 1977, Nike founded Athletics West Track Club in Eugene, Oregon. They signed up as many of the top American athletes as they could and hired Ilopo Nikkoli, a Finnish masseur to look after these athletes. Over the next few years, his work with the top American athletes convinced Americans – and eventually just about everyone else – of the value of massage for athletes:

- He helped their injuries heal more quickly.
- His treatments were deemed to prevent injuries occurring.
- His athletes won everything in sight from sprints to marathons.

Sports massage finally came into its own with the advent of its inclusion as part of the medical provision at the Los Angeles XXIII Olympiad. One of the leading forces behind the acceptance of sports massage at the Olympic Games was the Sports Massage Training Institute of Costa Mesa, California and its Principal, Dr. Myk Hungerford.

Dr. Hungerford presented a five-day intensive at the Northern Institute in 1998 and it is partly Dr. Hungerford's pre-event procedures that I will describe. The remainder of the techniques have been developed and taught by Northern Institute tutors and practitioners over many years.

The Aims of Pre-activity Massage

The aims of pre-activity massage are to bring about an improvement in:

- Speed;
- Power;
- Endurance;
- Flexibility;
- Readiness (including a relaxed mind), and;
- Be an aid to injury prevention.

The effects of the techniques employed by the therapist are several. To:

- Improve cellular nutrition through the dilation of capillaries by the use of deep compressions.
- Stimulate lymphatic flow thus milking waste products from the tissues.
- Break up any minor adhesions with deep transverse friction.
- Improve the circulation to tendons and ligaments with deep transverse or circular frictions.
- Release fibrous areas in muscles.
- Remove tightness out of tense muscles that are often shortened and tight as the result of previous training.

Thus the dancer should be able to perform at peak level and with the chances of injury decreased.

The Techniques of Pre-activity Massage

I will discuss Dr. Hungerford's style of pre-activity massage first. These techniques have the advantage of being able to be used through clothing, e.g. dance practise wear or costumes. The essence of this style of massage is a pattern of deep compressions to the belly of a muscle and transverse frictions to the attachments, that is, the origins and insertions of the muscles.

How to Apply the Techniques

The compressions to the belly of a muscle are given by the therapist's dominant hand that is reinforced by the other hand. The compressions should be administered rhythmically and progressively deeper with each set. Normally three sets of compression to a muscle belly are given, followed by three sets of transverse frictions. The therapist must work within the dancer's pain tolerance and depth can be obtained by progression from one set to the next.

Contra-indication to Pre-dance Massage

This form of massage treatment must only be given to strong, healthy persons. It is too powerful for the frail, the elderly and the already injured. I repeat, do not give this type of massage treatment to anyone with an injury.

Compressions

The muscle tissue is compressed with the palm of the hand and released with a 'sucking' motion. It is easier to use the dominant hand to make the contact with the muscle belly and to reinforce the movement with the

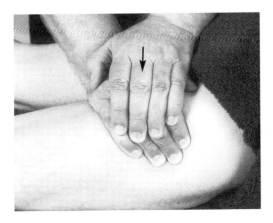
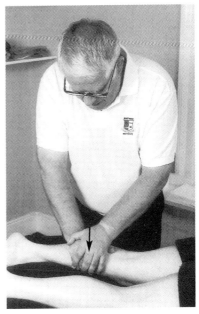

▲ ▶ *Figure 2.1:*
Compression to the muscle belly.

other hand, thus giving a two-handed compression. This technique, applied three times to a particular muscle belly, performs several functions, including spreading the muscle fibres and intensifying blood supply.

Transverse or Crossfibre Frictions

The transverse frictions are applied with the fingertips or with the thumb. The frictions may cause some local, low-level soreness in the tissues that may last up to a day or two but the longer-term effects far outweigh the short-term soreness. Local transverse friction strokes to connective tissue generally leaves no soreness.

The purposes of transverse frictions are to loosen and re-align scar tissue and adhesions from tendons and tendon sheaths, to render scar tissue more pliable and less likely to irritate the surrounding tissues, thus reducing the likelihood of re-injury. The frictions accomplish this by helping create a fibrillory network within the scar tissue itself. Please remember that this type of treatment is not advised over a new injury.

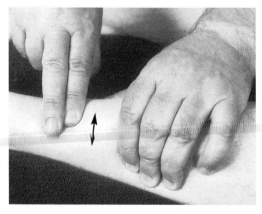

◄ ▲ *Figure 2.2:*
Crossfibre frictions to the Achilles tendon.

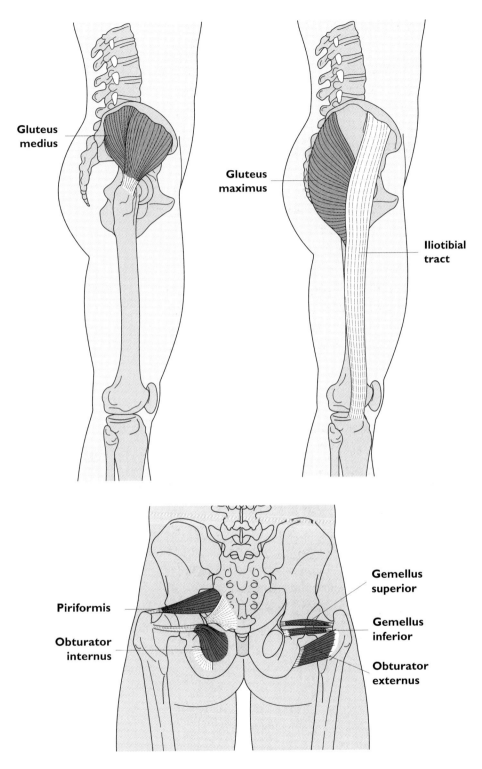

▲ Figure 2.3:
Gluteus maximus, gluteus medius and piriformis.

Optimum Time for Pre-dance Massage

Pre-dance massage is part of the warm up routine and is best applied during the forty-five minutes prior to the training session or dance. It is effective any time during the pre-dance hours but best during the warm-up session.

A Treatment Sequence for Legs and Hips

Time: *5–7 minutes*

Gluteals

Compressions to gluteus maximus and medius
Transverse friction to the muscular attachments
Transverse friction across belly of piriformis
3 sets

Posterior Legs

Compressions to bellies of hamstrings
Deep transverse friction to origins and insertions of hamstrings
Compressions to bellies of gastrocnemius and soleus
Transverse friction to Achilles tendon
3 sets

Plantar Foot

Thumb compressions to plantar surface of foot
Transverse friction of metatarsal heads
Transverse friction across origin of plantar fascia at calcaneum
3 sets

Anterior Legs

Compressions of quadriceps and tensor fasciae latae
Transverse friction of origins and insertions of rectus femoris, sartorius and tensor fasciae latae
3 sets

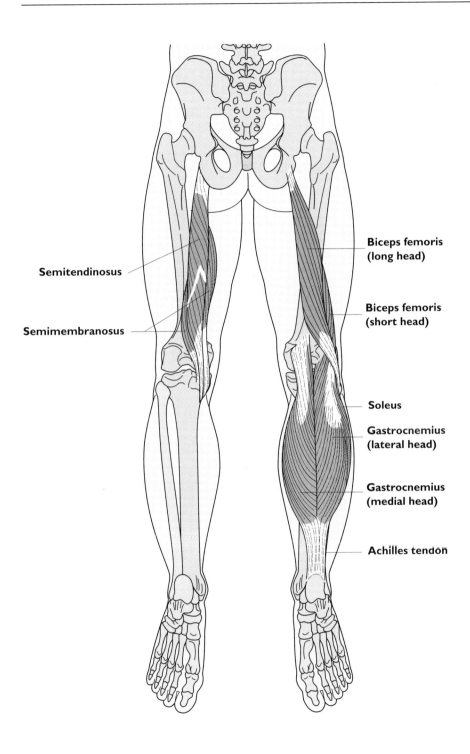

Semitendinosus

Semimembranosus

Biceps femoris
(long head)

Biceps femoris
(short head)

Soleus

Gastrocnemius
(lateral head)

Gastrocnemius
(medial head)

Achilles tendon

▲ *Figure 2.4:*
The hamstrings, gastrocnemius, soleus and Achilles tendon.

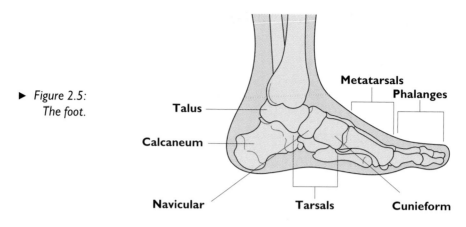

► *Figure 2.5:*
The foot.

Talus

Calcaneum

Metatarsals

Phalanges

Navicular

Tarsals

Cunieform

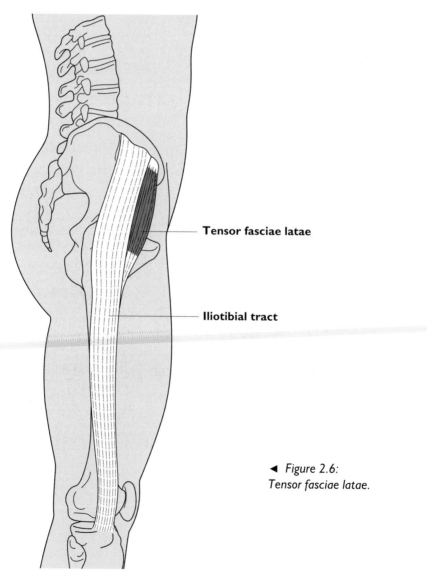

Tensor fasciae latae

Iliotibial tract

◄ *Figure 2.6:*
Tensor fasciae latae.

A Treatment Sequence for Neck and Back

Time: *4–7 minutes*

Occiput

Transverse friction to base
3 sets

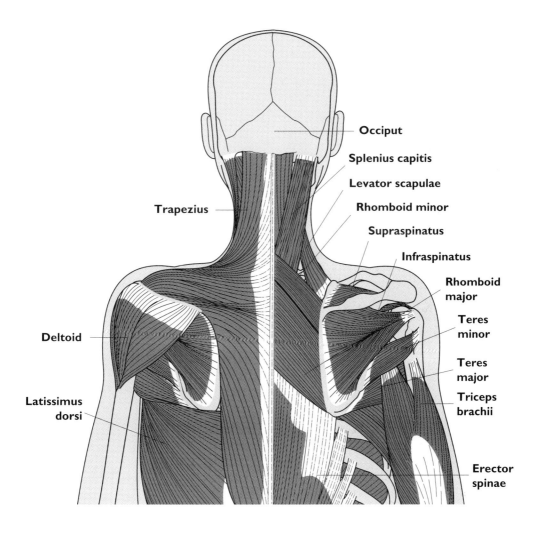

▲ *Figure 2.7:*
The upper back muscles.

Compressions to bellies of;
Upper trapezius
Supraspinatus
Infraspinatus
Posterior deltoid
Teres minor and major
Latissimus dorsi
Rhomboideus minor and major
3 sets

Transverse friction to attachments of;
Supraspinatus
Levator scapulae
Rhomboideus minor and major (at vertebral border of scapulae)
Infraspinatus
Teres minor and major
Latissimus dorsi
3 sets

Transverse friction to attachments of;
Erector spinae around the sacro-iliac joints
3 sets

Compressions to gluteals
Transverse friction around gluteals

These techniques may be applied to muscle groups
not included in these schedules.

Pre-dance Techniques by Remedial Massage

These techniques are based upon traditional massage strokes practiced in the UK before the relatively newer American techniques. The techniques have the same aims and very similar effects on the body.

Contra-indication to Pre-dance Massage

This method of massage treatment should only be used on healthy bodies and not on the frail, elderly or recently injured.

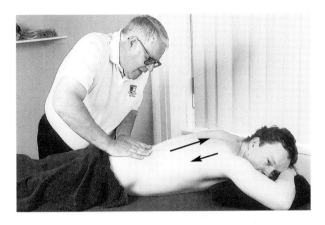

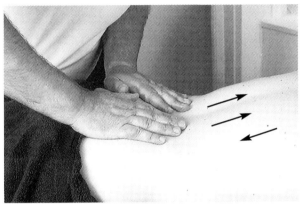

◄ *Figure 2.8:*
Effleurage – the start
position for back massage.

Effleurage

The effleurage stroke is employed in a much quicker movement and the hands are used to produce a compressive effect on the muscle, hence this is sometimes referred to as 'compressive effleurage'. For example, effleurage of the hamstrings would consist of no more than six or seven rapid applications in which the hands stroke and grasp progressively deeper.

Petrissage

The same movements of petrissage are used; lifting, lifting and squeezing, lifting and rolling, wringing and kneading. They are performed increasingly firmly and much more quickly than usual in a remedial or restorative massage. For example, petrissage of the bellies of the hamstring would consist of six or seven strokes of each of the techniques performed progressively deeper and firmer.

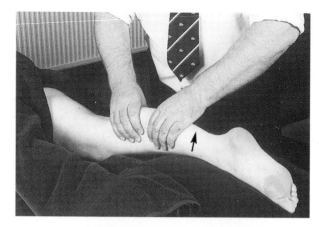

► Figure 2.9: Petrissage of the lower leg.

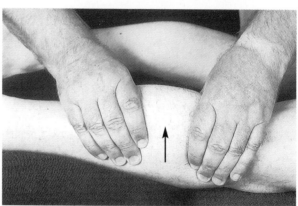

► Figure 2.10: Lifting and squeezing of the muscle.

Muscle 'Spreading' or 'Broadening'

This technique, described by King (1993) is similar to the movement of lateralising in remedial massage. The hands firmly spread the muscle being treated from the middle outwards in each direction and then the muscle is drawn together again by the hands in a lighter stroke. This is repeated six or seven times.

Tapotement

Clapping and hacking may each be performed for a short period of 10–15 seconds on each muscle or muscle group. The therapist may use these techniques as part of the dancer's preparation for practise or performance. The techniques can be applied to any muscle or muscle groups and will have a similar effect to the procedure of muscle belly compression and transverse friction. The treatment is of brief duration, 5–7 minutes and the application is brisk and stimulating.

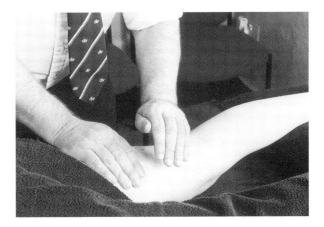

► *Figure 2.11:*
Tapotement of the
hamstrings – clapping.

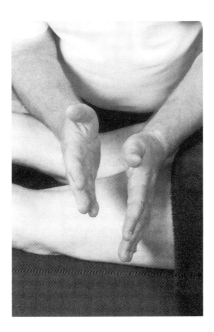

◄ ▲ *Figure 2.12:*
Tapotement of the hamstrings – hacking –
using the ulnar edge of the hands.

Inter-dance Massage

A dancer may be required to perform several times during a one- or two-day period or may have a busy and active college schedule. Inter-dance massage will help meet the dancer's needs in the period, however brief, between activities. The dancer is recovering from one performance and preparing for another and thus the treatment sessions are quite short and combine a little from the pre-dance massage and a little from the post-dance massage routines.

The massage is brief and of a lighter application than the pre-dance massage. It should focus on areas that may need immediate attention at that time, for example, perhaps the dancer may complain of a feeling of tightness in a hamstring muscle or in the calf muscles. The aims should be to improve the circulation for better nutritional supply and removal of waste products left over from the last performance. The therapist must avoid deep and painful techniques.

Guidelines for Inter-dance Massage

- The treatment should last for between 4–10 minutes, and;
- Should not be painful.
- The emphasis should be on the muscle groups
  most used in the performance.
- Look for any areas of tension resulting from the last performance.
- Help the dancer relax and prepare mentally for the next performance.

In the case of very short periods of time between dances, e.g. 10 minutes, simple petrissage-type movements can be used, without oil and through the dancer's clothing if required. Another example may be of direct muscle belly pressure by the therapist's thumb or fingers to a tight muscle.

Post-dance Massage – the Warm down

After dancing, whatever the circumstances, the importance of a warm down cannot be overemphasised whether the dancer is a novice or a professional performer. The warming down session is as important as the warming up session before dancing. It is done perhaps more gently and will probably be of shorter duration, e.g. 12–15 minutes.

Massage may be included in the dancers' warm down. Massage is helpful in several ways.

- To more quickly clear away toxic wastes that inevitably build up during the vigorous physical activity of dancing.
- The redistribution of blood and prevents 'pooling', thus improving recovery time and decreasing the risk of injury.

- Relieve muscle stiffness and physical tension. Dancers claim less muscle soreness on the day after if warm down and/or massage is practiced.
- Massage after dancing may help identify areas of micro trauma to the therapist and early remedial treatment may begin.
- Reduce tension and upset in the event of a competition that was not won, or even after a disappointing session.

Post-dance Massage Treatments

As we have just discussed, massage may be incorporated into the dancer's warm down routine. However, the post-dance session may require much more than a relaxing massage. The post-dance phase may be defined under several different headings and the procedure for treating the dancer may change quite dramatically depending upon their needs.

Warm down Massage

The warm down massage is a short session of between 12–15 minutes with the aim of helping the dancer relax after the efforts and demands of the activity and to allow the body to ease back to normal functioning as outlined above.

The massage may start with the dancer lying face down on the treatment table and, with the exception of the area being treated, covered by towels to prevent too rapid a cooling-off. A slower effleurage than that used in the pre-dance massage is employed to relax and gently ease the major muscle groups of the legs, hips, back and neck and shoulder areas of the dancer's body.

This will be followed by the petrissage techniques, again performed more slowly than in the pre-dance treatment. The aims are to ease the wastes out of the tissues whilst encouraging the flow of nutrition bearing, oxygenated blood to the tissue.

The dancer should then be turned to lie on her back, again covered by the towels except for the part of the body under treatment and the massage is continued to the front of the leg and the thigh.

The therapist does not use any of the techniques outlined in the pre-dance massage, but the opportunity to examine whilst massaging is taken. The therapist is able to palpate the various muscle groups and around the joints to find any areas of tenderness, soreness or pain. If any are discovered, the emphasis of the treatment changes away from a quiet warm down to the remedial situation which we will discuss shortly.

Chapter 3
The Causes of Injuries, First Aid and Acute Injuries

Injuries may be caused by any one of a number of factors, or, indeed, by a combination of several of them. Howse and Hancock (1988) highlighted some of these:

Anatomical causes: the dancer has certain physical limitations that may play a part in preventing the development of a perfect technique, e.g. limited external rotation at the hips.

Lack of technical knowledge: young dancers will be prone to injuries whilst trying to put into effect the techniques they are in the process of learning.

Poor teaching: some teachers do not understand the limitations of their students and may push them too far too soon or may fail to notice faults in technique that will lead to injury. Howse and Hancock illustrate this with the cases of teachers who put children on pointe too early.

Non-application of correct technique: this includes dancers at the highest level who, on occasions, do not use the correct technique, especially when tired. Many performances in a short period, travel, insufficient rest added to deteriorating technique will lead to injury.

The young or beginner dancer is susceptible to injury due to muscles, tendons and ligaments not being strengthened enough for the demands made upon them. Often the forces applied to these tissues and structures are greater than their inherent strength. Pre-dance massage will help the young or beginner dancer overcome the effects more easily.

More experienced or professional dancers tend to have problems related to overuse and fatigue. Muscles (and other tissues) may not be given sufficient time to recover normally from vigorous or even punishing treatment. Severe muscle injuries occur when muscles have been taxed so heavily that they lose the ability to relax and stretch out;

"In the normal action of dancing, the leg stretches out as it strikes the ground or floor. As the foot strikes, the hamstrings contract to initiate flexion of the knee. If the quadriceps, through fatigue, fail to release, the hamstrings will suffer injury and tear due to the greater strength of the quadriceps. Newly strained muscles should never be heavily stretched or even massaged in the acute stage of an injury. Injured fibres do not regenerate and healing will be slow and, sometimes, incomplete. This is especially true of dancers who are unwilling to rest, allowing their injury to heal or fatigue to ease before the next session."

To dance well, the body must be able to flow uninhibited through any given motion that a dance requires. Any inhibition will cause a drop-off in performance. Only when a movement is in perfect synchronisation may optimum performance be obtained. A few relatively small muscular problems in various areas of the body may work together to destroy freedom of movement and prevent optimum performance.

A dancer may experience tenderness say, in an Achilles tendon during a performance. To protect the Achilles tendon, the dancer tends to use the calf muscles less and the hamstrings more. If the demands of the performance are not reduced, the hamstrings will also become injured. If the dancer continues, the injuries become worse and the dancer becomes 'one-legged' and the performance dips considerably.

Muscle fibres work in unison; if several fibres are injured and rendered useless, the overall strength and efficiency of the muscle is diminished. This has been demonstrated many times by strength tests to injured areas of the body.

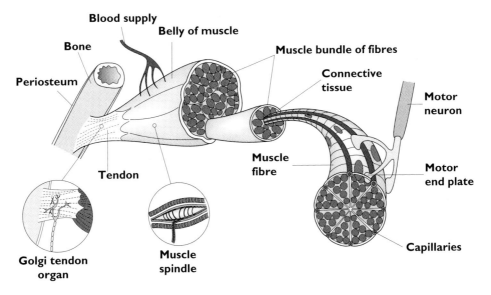

▲ Figure 3.1:
Skeletal muscle fibre.

Strength may be increased through corrective exercises to that particular area but, if the fibres are untreated, the strength gained will quickly diminish. The reason is that, although the remaining fibres improve, the cause of the weakness has not been treated. Once the corrective exercises cease, the cause will resurface again, perhaps not immediately, but eventually this will occur. We need to allow injured fibres, healing by scar tissue formation, the opportunity to relax so that they too may take part in normal contraction. When this happens, coordination, synchrony, and improved movement is back.

Over-activity produces muscle fatigue. Fatigue is reached when waste is greater than repair. This waste is made up chiefly of acids and these acids may be found separately or in combination in the form of carbonites in the muscles which have reached exhaustion. Muscular fatigue can be greatly relieved by massage. It is a well-established fact that massage helps increase the flow of lymph and the waste product it carries from the tissues (Hungerford, 1993).

Several hours after a hard dance session, muscle soreness sets in. The better the condition of the dancer, the less severe the soreness will be as the musculature can sustain higher workloads without breaking down. Soreness, often referred to as Delayed Onset Muscle Soreness (or

D.O.M.S.) takes several hours to surface because of the slow process of repair to injured tissue. Massage is a very efficient and relieving form of treatment for this condition.

First Aid and Acute Injuries

On occasions, a dancer may suffer a serious injury and, in the absence of a doctor or a qualified First Aider, the massage therapist must take control of the situation. All massage therapists, and especially those who treat dancers and athletes, should possess a valid First Aid qualification. The therapist must know how to react to any situation in which serious injury may occur.

There are a number of conditions in which urgent medical attention is required, for example:

- Unconsciousness, persistent headache, nausea, vomiting or dizziness after a head injury.
- Breathing difficulties, especially after trauma to head, neck or chest.
- Pains in the neck after an impact incident.
- Abdominal pain after an injury situation.
- Blood in the urine after injury.
- Obvious or suspected fracture.
- Severe (or suspected) joint or ligament injury.
- Joint dislocation or suspected dislocation.
- Eye injuries.
- Deep wound with bleeding.
- Any injury with intense unremitting pain.
- Any injury with doubts about the severity, diagnosis or treatment.
- A patient reporting that 24–36 hours after an injury they have severe, persisting symptoms.
- Suspected cardiac arrest.

In situations where a dancer, a member of staff or a member of the public sustain what is apparently a serious and possibly life-threatening injury, the therapist must make up his mind and act immediately. Do not delay, either phone for the emergency services, or order a reliable person to do so while you attend to the patient.

For example, in the case of a cardiac patient, it is imperative that you make sure the call to the emergency services is made as soon as possible. Then place the patient on their back and raise the legs. Check that the airway is clear; tilt the head back and, if necessary, physically clear the airway with your fingers. Start mouth to mouth resuscitation. Now check the patient's pulse. If the pulse is absent, start chest compressions. Combine two mouth to mouth inflations with fifteen chest compressions. If the patient is breathing, turn them into the recovery position.

This may seem a little extreme in a book about dance injuries, but often the therapist attends performances that attract an audience. The therapist, as a first aid measure, may have to treat members of the audience who become ill. I recall discussing this very situation with a sports massage therapist who once attended a regional athletics championship meeting that drew a very large crowd. By sheer chance and bad planning, he was the only person in the stadium with any kind of medical background for a period of three hours. During that time, he was called upon to deal with athletes' injuries, plus several faints, an epileptic seizure, a patient with a suspected heart attack and a pregnant spectator who went into labour.

Hence the statement about First Aid training earlier. The therapist is not looking to take over the duties of the recognised First Aider, but to be prepared to deal with the unexpected in a professional, safe and effective manner.

Head injuries, for example the result of a collision between two dancers, require the utmost professional care and a referral to a GP or an Accident and Emergency Unit may be the appropriate course of action.

The therapist must check for the following:

- Dizziness and/or loss of coordination after the injury.
- Temporary loss of memory and/or confusion.
- Severe, deep throbbing headaches.
- Blurred or double vision after the incident.
- Ringing noises in the dancer's ears.
- Unequal pupil size.
- Lack of pupil reaction to light.
- Slurred speech.

- Convulsions or tremors.
- Nausea and vomiting.
- Sleepiness or grogginess.
- If asleep, any difficulty in being woken.
- Fluid seeping from nose and/or ears.
- Any partial or complete paralysis or numbness.

The injured dancer should be checked at frequent intervals, e.g. every two hours for breathing rate, heart rate and colour. After sustaining such an injury, the dancer should only be given clear liquid to drink and should not be given any medication unless instructed by a doctor. Get medical help as a matter of urgency – do not leave anything to chance.

Concussion is a bruising of part of the brain as the result of a blow to the head or a severe shaking of the body. Cases vary in severity from a mere sense of temporary dizziness and headache for an hour or two to a complete loss of consciousness which may last for weeks and may include loss of memory for facts and events and even of personal identity. Firstly, the therapist cannot diagnose the condition or the severity. He may be able to hazard a guess but that is not good enough. In some cases, the symptoms do not appear until some hours have elapsed and the injured dancer may be miles away and quite alone by that time. What at first glance may appear to be a mild case may develop in the next few minutes or the next few hours into a serious condition.

The therapist should not allow dancers with post trauma headaches to return to the activity. A mere bump on the head will appear as a trivial external injury; what is happening inside the head may be much more serious. Get expert medical help for the dancer with a head injury.

The basic responsibilities of the therapist in these situations are to:

- Assess the situation.
- Offer immediate, appropriate and adequate treatment.
- Be fully responsible for the patient until that patient is handed over to a doctor, paramedic, nurse, etc.
- Maintain your knowledge and skills, e.g. have a valid certificate of first aid competence.

The Acute Stage of a Minor Injury

The dancer reports pain, discomfort, stiffness or a restriction of movement when she reports to the massage therapist after dancing. The therapist does not rush to massage the injury but rather conducts an examination of the patient. Early injury recognition and appropriate immediate follow-up care are crucial to effective injury management (Arnheim, 1999).

Examination of the patient is by several methods and, at the end of the session, the therapist should know much more about the patient's condition and if the patient's condition requires that the patient will have to be referred to their doctor or to the hospital.

Examination of the Injured Dancer

The dancer should be invited to sit down and asked about the injury. Some patients will readily give an articulate and intelligent account of the incident or the circumstances. Others may have to be led by skilful questioning, for example:

"Tell me just what happened."
"Where does it hurt?"
"What is the pain like?"
"When did you hurt yourself?"
"Have you had this kind of injury before?"

In other words, the therapist is trying to get the patient's account of the problem. As well as this, the therapist must find out about the patient's previous medical record and the current state of the patient's health. The secret to conducting this part of the examination is to sit and listen and remember what the patient says and, when needed, gently direct the patient by the skilled use of questions.

The therapist must always use his eyes and see what information he can collect from looking at the patient's general demeanour, how the patient walks, sits, takes garments off, watch the facial expressions as well as the general body language. By watching and looking at the patient, the therapist will be able to gather quite a lot of information about the patient and the patient's injury. A more formal visual examination of the patient may take place in the next stage of the examination.

The patient may next be required to remove a garment or two so that the therapist can continue with the visual and palpatory examinations. In these cases the patient must be afforded the use of a screen or changing area and also be allowed to cover any parts of the body not being examined by towels. The procedure must be fully explained to the patient and the patient's permission and approval must be obtained before progressing further with the examination.

The visual examination continues with a careful look at the injured area of the body and a comparison with a corresponding uninjured part. For example, if the patient is complaining of a knee pain, the therapist should visually examine both the injured knee and the uninjured knee.

The therapist will look for any unusual signs such as swelling or bruising or a change of shape and this is where an examination of the uninjured part is valuable. After looking, the therapist will palpate or try to examine by the sense of touch. He will feel the injured knee or ankle and, as with the visual examination, he will also feel any comparable uninjured part. Again, he will be feeling to find a difference in shape, or texture or temperature; in short, anything that may give information about the injury.

The final part of the examination procedure is to conduct an examination by movement. This is to get the patient to move the injured part and find out which movements are painful or restricted and to replicate the movements that caused the injury in the first place. This may be done by the patient actively moving the injured area and also by the therapist moving the injured part for the patient; examination by active and passive movements.

At the conclusion of the examination procedure, the therapist should be able to ascertain if the patient is suffering from a muscle injury or a joint injury. Together with this he should have information about the patient and the patient's medical state. Are there any contra-indications to treatment by massage? If there are none and the therapist remains happy with the assessment of the patient after the examination, the next step is to discuss the results of the assessment and to plan an appropriate course of treatment for the patient.

Delayed Onset Muscle Soreness (D.O.M.S.)

The results of the examination will guide the therapist to the treatment required by each patient. After a particularly hard session, the dancer may not have sustained an injury as such but may begin to display symptoms of delayed onset muscle soreness or D.O.M.S. By definition, this condition is not immediately apparent and may not manifest itself until some hours after the activity.

This condition usually happens to dancers who are not in as good a physical condition as they should be for the demands that they make upon their muscles. It may be that they have had a long lay-off from dancing and come back with an arduous practise session. It may be that they unusually dance for a lot longer or at a greater intensity than usual. The result is very noticeable the next day; pain and stiffness in the affected muscles.

Skeletal muscle that is over-exerted may suffer from this delayed onset muscle soreness especially if that muscle or group of muscles has not been exercised in that particular manner for a period of time prior to the dance session. A number of studies have described the tenderness in terms of its locality; it is generally in the distal portion of the muscle near the junction of muscle and tendon (*see* figure 3.1, page 39). In more extreme cases, the whole of the muscle may exhibit tenderness and stiffness for some days. D.O.M.S. occurs in the following. The:

- New dancer who has little experience of dance movements.
- More experienced dancer who performs a completely new and vigorous activity.
- Experienced dancer who over-exerts on normal activities.
- Dancer who undertakes a completely new type of activity, e.g. training with weights, in which there are eccentric (muscle lengthening) exercises.

The probable causes of muscle soreness after exercise are micro tears in muscle fibres and damage to the connective tissues leading to an influx of fluid, causing pressure and the normal inflammatory response, causing pain. This type of muscle pain is experienced at some time or another by most people and may last for up to three weeks in severe cases. The symptoms are:

- 1–3 hours after dancing. Evidence of some form of motor impairment, aches and possibly cramps, feelings of fatigue.
- 1–3 days after dancing. Stiffness, weakness and pain on movement. This is the most painful period.
- 3–21 days after dancing. Tenderness on palpation, decreasing pain but perhaps still noted on resisted movements, stiffness decreases.

Treatment for D.O.M.S.

Movement helps. A warm down after the activity that caused the condition would have helped minimise the effects. However, the dancer who experiences the symptoms of D.O.M.S. will feel an improvement from gentle, warming up type of activities. Massage to the areas affected will also hasten the removal of waste from the muscles and will allow an earlier (usually the same day) return to normal activities. Therapists receive many reports from their patients about the success of massage in these instances and the patients compare the situation to how they were on other occasions when they did not receive massage.

Massage is very effective for new dancers and for more experienced and older dancers who feel they are experiencing this condition. Massage will allow the dancer to return to normal dancing activities much more quickly.

Treatment of Musculoskeletal Injuries

During the acute stage, musculoskeletal injuries, e.g. a hamstring muscle strain or a sprained medial knee ligament, would be treated by the R.I.C.E.S formula:

R   Rest.
I   Ice.
C   Compression.
E   Elevation.
S   Stabilisation.

Rest

The injured dancer should rest from any activity that aggravates the condition further. If it hurts to perform an action, then the dancer must not perform. Dancing through an injury will make the original injury worse, will slow down the healing processes and may become a chronic or permanent condition that may bring a premature end to a dancer's career.

Ice (or Cold Therapy)

The use of ice is well documented and it is generally agreed that the correct application of ice to an acute injury will help the healing processes. Most vessels injured during dancing will seal themselves within a few minutes of the injury happening. Ice limits secondary damage rather than being used just to stop haemorrhaging. It limits an increase in fluid pressure by lowering metabolism and decreases the secondary effect of the injury, limiting the amount of tissue debris (Basur, et al., 1992).

Crushed ice, which is at $0°C$, is recommended. It should be applied for approximately twenty minutes every two hours for the first seventy-two hours of the injury. Other variations of this formula are to be found in other texts but it is expedient to use ice at this temperature rather than a chemical pack or a bag of frozen peas direct from the freezer. The temperature of these may well be considerably below $-3.9°C$ – the level at which frostbite occurs. Thus, it is advisable not to place the ice directly onto the skin but to enclose it in some form of wrapping to protect the patient. The therapist should check with the patient to see if they are hypersensitive to ice.

Compression

Compression is beneficial in limiting and controlling oedema during the acute stage of injury and should be used at the same time as the ice treatment. The therapist must take extra care in advising and supervising patients who are at this stage of injury. The incorrect application of compression can do much more harm than good.

Elevation

Elevation of an injured limb or body part during the acute stage of the injury is recommended. Some limbs and body parts are easier to elevate than others but it helps decrease capillary pressure.

Stabilisation

Stabilisation refers to the use of strapping, taping, a sling or walking stick to assist with the treatment, help limit pain and prevent unnecessary movement. Neither rest, compression nor stabilisation requires that the patient is immobilised.

Immobilisation affects the drainage away from the injured part, causes atrophy, and inhibits neural responses, thus lengthening the healing period and, possibly, creating even more problems for the patient. For example, there is a variety of receptors in joints, tendons, ligaments and muscles which respond to mechanical stress and movement. Impulses from these are supplemented by similar mechanoceptors in the skin.

- Muscle spindles measure tension and stretch and feed into a spindle reflex, e.g. sudden stretching fires off the spindle and causes a reflex muscle contraction.
- Golgi bodies at musculo-tendon junctions measure tension.
- Pacinian corpuscles in the periosteum, interosseous membranes and deeper layer soft joint capsules respond to mechanical disturbance.
- Free nerve endings inside joints are stimulated by excessive movement and pressure causing pain.

The inhibition of these responses due to immobilisation leads to a much longer recovery period than if some movement is encouraged in the acute stage of the injury.

Massage During the Acute Stage of the Injury

Massage may be contra-indicated at this stage of the injury, certainly at the site of the problem because it would impede the recovery process and do more harm than good. The RICES formula should be followed as the treatment of choice. Massage above the site of the injury may be beneficial in stimulating drainage away from the injury in conjunction with the other aspects of the treatment.

Restorative Massage for a 'Tired' Dancer

Massage after dancing may be applied to the dancers' legs or to the whole body. The therapist will be seeking to ease and relax the dancer. In other words, to assist the drainage of blood and lymph from the muscles and to ease any minor aches and pains that resulted from the dance session.

The full body massage will take approximately sixty minutes whereas a full massage to the legs will take between twenty and twenty-five minutes. The massage will be of effleurage, petrissage and frictions with some variations of each, for example muscle broadening and lateralising. The therapist will start quite gently and superficially and work increasingly deeper but within the individual's tolerance.

The massage session should include mobilising of the major joints, e.g. the shoulders, and stretching of the main muscles and muscle groups. Ideally, a busy dancer should receive regular, perhaps daily, restorative massage treatments. Colleagues who work with Premiership soccer clubs report that many players, especially those who have played in European leagues, stipulate daily massage treatment in their contracts. The busy dancer makes similar demands upon the body.

Treating Cramp

Muscle cramping is likely to occur during a long session. Dehydration may be a factor, especially in warm conditions. Dancers should drink plenty of water or 'replacement' drinks before, during and probably after long sessions or when dancing in humid or hot conditions. Cramping in muscles can be relieved by several methods:

1. Direct pressure into the belly of the affected muscle. Use the hand, fist or forearm to apply pressure to the appropriate place.
2. Gently stretch the affected muscle and hold in the stretch position, until the cramp subsides.
3. Approximation will help relax the muscle. To achieve this, the therapist grasps the muscle belly on either side of the cramped area and pushes his hands towards each other and holds for about 10 seconds. Then, as the muscle relaxes, apply a gentle stretch.
4. What is the antagonist muscle of the muscle in cramp? Engage this muscle in an isometric contraction that should trigger a reciprocal inhibition and relaxation of the muscle in spasm.
5. Use ice or massage followed by a mild stretch.

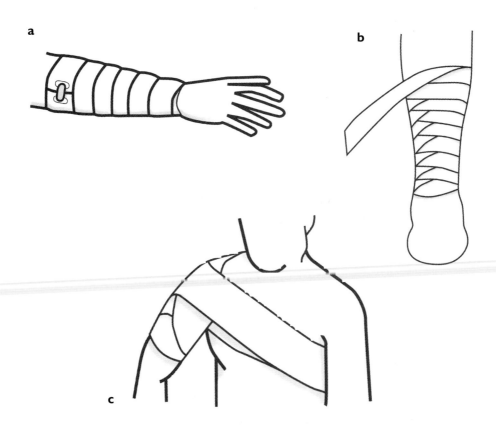

▲ *Figure 3.2:*
Some common strapping techniques,
(a) circular or simple spiral; (b) reverse spiral, and; (c) spica.

The Use of Strappings and Supports

Taping, bandaging and strappings are used to provide support for the tissues of an injured limb or a joint to allow for some movement in the pain-free ranges of movement but to limit movement in the painful range. Strapping is a temporary arrangement and, as Petersen and Renstrom (1986) pointed out, not a permanent solution to the problem. An important rule to observe is that the therapist must know what he is strapping and why he is doing it; otherwise do not use strapping. When used for the correct reasons and in the correct manner, tapings and strappings can be very useful. The reverse is also true; when used for the wrong reasons or in an incorrect way, strappings, tapings and supports can be harmful. When in doubt, leave it out (Briggs, 2000).

Athletes, dancers included, should not participate until the healing process is complete enough for them to dance without tape, and so it is not a good idea to strap a part, e.g. an ankle, to permit an activity which would otherwise cause pain. Dancers and athletes should be able to participate without the use of yards of taping (Dornan and Dunn, 1987). Grisogono (1984) pointed out that the pain is a sure sign that the ankle is not ready for use, and so it would be wrong to permit activity. If the ankle is immobilised and then the activity is resumed, there are bound to be repercussions to the knee and probably the hip and back also. The use of strapping should be limited to as short a period of time as possible because of the negative effects that longer-term strapping will have on other tissues, e.g. muscles, ligaments.

Thus, if an injury makes dancing painful, the dancer should stop dancing and allow the injury to heal rather than bind the injury in an attempt to ease the pain. If the joint is completely immobilised by the strapping, the risks increase and not only is ankle movement interfered with, but there will be a knock-on effect to knee, hip and back movement that may result in more extensive injury.

Sperryn (1983) considered that strapping was worthwhile, mainly for the fact that it would allow some movement of the injured part and would maintain the proprioceptive or positional awareness of the joint. He gave the example of the ankle where it increases the rate at which the proprioceptive or positional sensory nerve fibres fire impulses just before the foot lands in walking, jumping or dancing. This enhanced response ensures that the correct neuromuscular preparations for landing are improved. He favoured the simple 'U' shaped stirrup strapping rather than the 'figure of eight' strapping that he claimed restricts up and down movement. Minter (1999) looked at the psychological or placebo effects of strapping and how this may help in the recovery from injury.

A therapist may use taping and strapping on dancers and sports people in the acute stage of an injury. The therapist will apply the strapping or taping for a specific purpose and for a limited period of time. Later on, as the patient resumes dancing or training, the therapist may again employ a strapping or method of taping to avoid the risk of re-injury to the joint or limb during the first few sessions. In some cases, this may prove to be more of a psychological help or a placebo to the patient who feels that the now recovered part is comfortable and secure.

Therapists may use strapping and taping purely to prevent an injury occurring. An example of preventative taping is in American (or Gridiron) Football where all the players in a team may have their ankles protectively taped to prevent ankle sprains. Sperryn commented upon the more adventurous use of strapping in American sport of that time compared with the more conservative outlook adopted in Britain.

Petersen and Renstrom (1986) questioned the use of strapping, for example, of the knee joint and the quadriceps muscles. The efficacy and benefits were, they thought, debatable. Incorrectly used, strapping, taping and supports can have detrimental effects on the efficiency of ligaments, muscles and tendons. The therapist should view their use in most cases as a short-term measure. There is little justification for a dancer or athlete to wear a taping or strapping around an injury for more than a week. The aim is that the strapping should support a weakened part of the body without limiting its function by preventing movements that stress the weakened area. This ideal is difficult to achieve even when the strapping is correctly applied.

Taping should not be used until the injury has been fully examined and assessed. Do not tape or strap a joint injury if the joint is swollen and painful; wait until the examination has been satisfactorily completed. The therapist should also find out if the patient is allergic to tape or plaster.

Skin irritation may also occur by mechanical or chemical means if it is left on for too long; allow a maximum of 3 days before changing or removing. The therapist must not use taping or strapping if he has any doubts about its value and if he is unsure about the techniques involved. When in doubt, leave it out.

Elastic bandages and tubigrip were according to Briggs (2000) the more effective types of strapping and perhaps the easiest to apply.

Chapter 4
Specific Injuries and Their Treatment by Massage

Recovery From Injury

Whatever the cause of the injury, dancers immediately want to know what is injured and how soon they can return to dancing. There are many factors involved in an injury and its healing process, so it is difficult to give an entirely accurate answer. There are a number of factors that influence recovery from injury:

- Generally, some tissues heal more quickly than others, for example, a damaged muscle heals more quickly than a broken bone which in turn may heal more quickly than an injured ligament.
- Younger people heal more quickly than older people; the healing process slows with increased age.
- Good health or chronic illness are factors for quicker or slower healing; even young patients with serious underlying health problems will take longer to heal.
- Similarly a good, healthy lifestyle will have an influence on healing; a healthy lifestyle will encourage quicker healing. Smokers, for instance, heal more slowly than comparable non-smokers.

The injured dancer and the therapist must both look at these factors when discussing the injury situation. Is the injury straightforward and without complications? What other factors may be involved that will slow down healing and recovery?

Bones, Muscles, Tendons and Ligaments

A broken bone repairs by the formation of callus, i.e. more bone forms to effect union and repair. Diagnosis and treatment of fractures is not within the sphere of expertise of the massage therapist. Once the fracture heals the skills of the therapist may be employed around the injured area.

Skeletal muscle has little capacity for regeneration and healing is by fibrosis or scar formation. Injuries to other connective tissues, e.g. tendons and ligaments heal in this way. For the first three days or so after injury, the forming scar tissue is weak and fragile and may easily be re-injured if the patient does not take care and heed advice. By the seventh day, metabolic activity is at its height and the defect in the tissue is rapidly filling. At twenty days the quantity of collagen present is maximal.

However, this highly vascular new scar tissue has little tensile strength and will tear easily and bleed profusely. It is richly innervated with sensory nerve endings and is sensitive to pressure and tension. Changes takes place as the scar tissue matures; at seven days the tissue is, as noted above, largely restored but has very little tensile strength. By twenty days after the injury, the thin, and weak fibroblasts of the early stages have been replaced by stronger ones and the scar shortens and the injury has recovered to around 80–95% of the original pre-injury state.

Ligaments and tendons go through the same kind of repair process except that the normal healing time takes about four months rather than three weeks. This is without additional complicating factors that may slow progress down. Most ligament and tendon injuries are partial injuries rather than a complete tear. A complete tear will require the skills of a surgeon to effect recovery, whereas partial tears usually recover quite well.

Early mobilisation leads to good linear scar formation, prevents loss of muscle tone and loss of proprioceptive responses and, thus, recovery is better. Repeated episodes involving injury to the same part or tissue result in chronic conditions with lumpy, excess and painful fibrous tissue.

Scar Tissue

The mature scar tissue that forms to repair the torn muscle is not like muscle tissue. Muscle tissue is extensible and elastic whereas the new scar tissue is inelastic and, although it will stretch a little if subjected to repeated pulling, it will, if immobilised, tend to contract slowly as it matures.

If a muscle repairs with a contracted, puckered scar it will give further trouble when exercise recommences. As the muscle stretches, it pulls on the scar tissue giving discomfort, tightness and impaired movement. Worse still, a tight scar is liable to tear, causing bleeding and inflammation with even more scar tissue formation. Again, this will lead to a chronic condition that will bring a restriction in the use of the muscle group, loss of range of movement and loss of strength.

Preventative Treatment

Chronic damage and all it entails may be prevented, by graded stretching and light active exercises during the healing phase. This will assist the scar tissue to form with its fibres parallel to the line of pull. Regular repeated graded stretching will allow the collagen fibres in the scar tissue to elongate and form a linear rather than a puckered scar. The ability to contract is there and presents little problem; the injured dancer must be taught to stretch gently and to make sure that the injured muscle is warmed up before subjecting it to a dancing session.

One type of injury or muscle tear that is slow to heal is when the muscle fibres tear at or near the insertion into the periosteum. This is the attachment on the outer layer of the bone to which the muscle inserts itself in order to 'work' the bone. Examples of this type of injury include the tennis elbow type of injury where the extensor muscles of the wrist attach to the lateral epicondyle of the elbow, or the adductor magnus and its insertion into the pubic bone. The healing is slow because the immature scar tissue is under continuous stress as the hand/arm and leg movements allow very little rest to the site of the injury. This may lead to quite a significant amount of further bleeding and the formation of a knot of chronically inflamed tissue. Rest from causative activity is essential in the treatment of this type of injury. Some other factors that can affect the healing process:

- If the injured area has a poor blood supply it may need some help to supply the required oxygen and nutrients to the actively metabolising granulation tissue and to speed up the formation of the repairing scar tissue. Ultrasound or other electrotherapy would be recommended.
- Infections delay healing; make sure that any infections are treated and cleared up as quickly as possible.
- Nutritional deficiencies will interfere with healing, e.g. a possible Vitamin C or zinc deficiency.
- The injured dancer may also be taking medication that may suppress repair or allow only slow and weak repair to take place. There are many documented 'horror' stories from the past of anti-inflammatory and pain-killing injections given to dancers and sport people that have resulted in permanent, long-term damage.
- Non-steroidal anti-inflammatory drugs may be helpful in the acute stage of an injury. The therapist would not prescribe the taking of such medication but should be aware if the patient has taken them.
- Exercise will help strengthen antagonist muscles and take some of the strain off the injured muscle. Along with graded stretching, it helps scar formation, maintains joint mobility, muscle balance and proprioceptive reflexes. General exercise maintains fitness and helps avoid apathy and depression that may accompany an injury.

Categories of Muscle Strain

There are three types of categories of muscle strain listed and described by Armour (1983).

1. *First degree strain:* This is a mild, slight reaction, no swelling and only slight spasm; some low level pain or discomfort. Rapid recovery and return to training in 7–10 days.

2. *Second degree strain:* This is a moderate injury in which there has been tearing of part of the muscle accompanied by pain, swelling, partial loss of function; active and resisted tests will be painful. Recovery, depending on other factors, may take 4–6 weeks.
3. *Third degree strain:* This involves the complete tearing of a muscle and accompanied by severe pain and swelling with major loss of function. Probably requiring the skills of a surgeon and a lot of after-care by the therapist. Recovery may take 4–6 months.

Achilles Tendinitis

Achilles tendinitis is quite a common injury often brought about by a sudden increase in workload. Sometimes the cause may be a structural problem, e.g. a dancer who over-pronates or who has a cavus foot. Suspicions of Achilles tendinitis brought about by these problems would be referred to a podiatrist for a bio-mechanical analysis. Unsuitable footwear may also be a contributing factor, such as too rigid a sole or too soft a heel counter. Upon examination, sufferers are often found to have tight calf muscles and hamstrings and a dancer who receives regular leg massage helps prevent the onset of injury.

Occasionally, there is a traumatic cause for this condition but more often it is of gradual onset. The dancer experiences discomfort after activity that gets gradually worse with dancing and even walking until the condition becomes too painful to allow normal movements.

The tendon may become red and swollen and will certainly be painful on palpation with the possibility of a painful nodule forming about 4–5cms above the insertion in the heel bone.

Treatment

After completion of the full examination process and if there are no contra-indications, treatment may begin. The immediate aim is to reduce the pain, the heat or redness and the swelling and the area should be cooled with crushed ice for twenty minutes every two hours during the first two days of treatment. The patient must rest from any activities that cause pain in the tendon. Do not grit your teeth and struggle through pain barriers. It may be a measure of your bravery and determination but it will not help the injury to heal.

If the therapist has the equipment, experience and qualification, pulsed ultrasound at 0.5W/cm² for four minutes each day will be beneficial, at this stage.

Effleurage and petrissage movements to the whole of the leg above the site of the injury may commence immediately but do not massage the Achilles tendon during the initial acute stage.

The treatment for the tendon is by 'stripping out', a more vigorous thumb pressure that can certainly be very uncomfortable the first time it is performed. Subsequent applications, interspersed with effleurage, are less uncomfortable. The therapist must be aware of the patient's pain tolerance and not exceed it. Further effleurage and petrissage is done after the stripping out of the tendon. *Enzyme Ice*, or a similar topical gel, applied over the injured surface of the Achilles tendon will help cool the inflammation and also act as an analgesic.

A small supportive pad of chiropody felt placed under the heel on the offending foot until the next treatment will help take the tension out of the painful tendon. I would ask the dancer to return in two days time for the next treatment, but if anything occurs that causes pain or alarm, to telephone immediately for an appointment.

How many treatments will this take to heal? How soon can I dance again? These are the two most common questions the therapist is asked about this kind of injury. We cannot give an accurate answer because there are so many factors to take into consideration. Factors like the age of the dancer, the general state of health, fitness and lifestyle of the dancer, other specific medical conditions and even specific medications may slow down the rate of healing.

Along with the massage and ultrasound and perhaps some heat treatment at home, the therapist will suggest some gentle stretching exercises for the calf muscle and some active mobilising exercises for the ankle joint. As the recovery gathers pace, the therapist may test the anterior muscles of the leg and decide that they may need strengthening to prevent a re-occurrence of the injury.

All things being equal, the relative severity of each case, the dancer complying with instructions and nothing out-of-the-ordinary occuring, a healthy young dancer should be recovered enough to resume practise after four or five treatments spread over fourteen to sixteen days. Try to rush the recovery and the chances are that a chronic, career-threatening condition will develop. Arnheim (1999) quoted an old saying common among dancers, "One day of practise missed, the dancer can tell; two days missed, the audience can tell." Many dancers will try to dance through an injury. Some will get away with doing this; many more will not. Musculoskeletal injuries are thought by Arnheim to be one of the main reasons why many potentially outstanding dancers are prevented from reaching the top of their chosen field. I would carry this a stage further and suggest that not allowing enough time for musculoskeletal injuries to heal properly is a major factor.

Plantar Fasciitis

The foot is a pedestal and a means of locomotion or movement. Under normal circumstances the foot is subjected to stress and trauma, on a daily basis. It is often cramped by footwear and crushed by bodyweight and certain types of activity, for example, sport and dancing which bring their own demands upon the structures and tissues of the feet.

The plantar fascia is a strong band of tough, rather inelastic tissue on the sole of the foot that extends from the heel to toes. The signs of plantar fasciitis appear as pain under the heel bone near its junction with the rest of the foot when dancing. The pain may become more frequent and more painful. First thing in the morning is a difficult time, too. The under part of the foot is painful and stiff, movement is difficult and painful but this improves a little after 15–20 minutes. The patient feels pain on palpation and it is painful to stand on tiptoe.

The cause of the condition is an injury that is common to both the fascia of the plantar muscles of the foot and the short toe flexors and their attachment at the calcaneum. The injury may be the result of the stresses of a take-off for a leap or a very sharp turning movement. People with overpronated feet are also susceptible to this injury as are those who persevere through long activities in shoes that do not give adequate support to the feet. I also believe that there is a causative link between

Achilles and calf muscle overuse and tightness with plantar fasciitis brought about by the sustained stresses exerted on the calcaneum by these tissues. I have reached this conclusion because in very many cases of plantar fasciitis, I have found on examination that the dancer has a lot of tension in the gastrocnemius and soleus muscles (*see* figure 2.4, page 27).

Treatment for plantar fasciitis includes rest from activities that cause the pain to re-appear under the foot. Also, ice and anti-inflammatory measures in the acute stage; massage, including crossfibre friction at the attachment area of the foot and lower leg every other day until the symptoms ease. Pulsed ultrasound given at each treatment session is beneficial until there is a noted improvement. The use of a heel pad, shaped a little like a broadened horseshoe, will relieve the weight of the body on the injury site during the acute stage.

The dancer and therapist should check that all shoes are suitable and will not contribute to re-injury. Collaboration with parents, dance teachers and coaches about the amount of dancing required should take place.

Heel Spur

Heel spur refers to a calcification or bony spur from the calcaneum that gives similar symptoms to plantar fasciitis and is thought by many to be an extension of plantar fasciitis that is either badly treated or not treated at all. Some cases of heel spur will respond to the same treatment regime as plantar fasciitis. However, dancers experiencing this type of painful condition (and massage therapists working with the dancers) should make sure that they are examined by a podiatrist who possesses the highly skilled examination procedures and techniques required for an expert diagnosis.

The Podiatrist

Massage therapists and podiatrists often work closely together for the benefit of the injured dancer. We have, for instance, enjoyed a close and harmonious relationship with the Department of Podiatry at University College in Salford since the days when it was the Northern College of Chiropody with its associate premises off Daisybank Road in Manchester, formerly the Manchester Foot Hospital.

Our patients have, over a period of twenty years, received first class treatment when referred to the College for examination and/or treatment. One form of treatment does not automatically exclude any other form of treatment and the cumulative effects of treatments by the massage therapist and the podiatrist are usually greater than the sum of the two individual parts. The massage therapist must not hesitate to refer patients who present with injuries and problems that are truly within the province of another professional.

'Shin Splints'

The often-used description 'shin splints' occurs in many spheres of activity, even Andy Cole of Manchester United and England went through quite a bad period with this type of injury when he first came to Old Trafford. Cole was (and still is) a superbly conditioned professional athlete with the best possible physical and medical care. If he can be affected by this problem, so can anyone else.

The term 'shin splints' is often loosely used to inappropriately describe all pains that occur in the lower leg between ankle and knee with special reference to the shinbone. The use of the term relates to a number of conditions including the following:

- Anterior tibial myotendinitis.
- Posterior tibial myotendinitis.
- Stress fractures of tibia and/or fibula.
- Tearing of the interosseous membrane.
- Anterior tibial tenosynovitis.
- Partial avulsions.

Symptoms of 'Shin Splints'

The most striking symptom is pain in the middle third or lower third of the tibial area. This usually comes on only after activity at first, but then during dancing as well. In severe cases, it hurts very much just to try and walk normally.

Even passive dorsiflexion with the big toe extended and the knee locked is painful. The extreme range of passive plantar flexion is painful. There is a marked decrease in the ranges of movements of the ankle. The dancer cannot perform active dorsiflexion to ten degrees and plantar flexion to forty-five degrees. These symptoms are accompanied by tightness in the calf muscles in most cases (*see* figure 4.2, page 68).

In dancers, the main injuries are to the muscles and associated connective tissue at the antero-lateral aspect of the lower leg. In many cases it is an overuse injury that develops in tissues that are not well enough conditioned to cope with the stresses to which they are subjected. Unusual or new or a sudden increase in activities on hard surface are often associated with the problem. Other causes may include unsuitable footwear, banked or uneven surfaces, a pre-existing foot or arch condition (refer to the podiatrist if this is suspected), a hip or knee injury that has a knock-on effect to the lower leg.

If the problem is with the bones or soft tissue attachments to bones an X-ray or more sophisticated examination will provide a diagnosis.

Treatment of 'Shin Splints'

The first consideration is a short-term rest from any activity that causes pain. Ice applications and a topical gel (*Enzyme Ice, Movelat, Lasonil*) during the first two days. Pulsed ultrasound may be indicated and four or five treatments on successive days should help.

▶ *Figure 4.1:*
Kneading of the tibialis anterior is an important part of shin splint treatment.

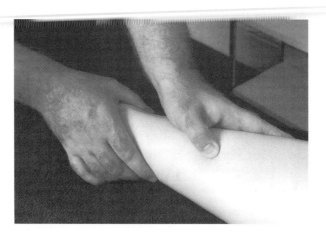

In the case of stress fractures, rest from painful activity is the main thrust of treatment. Stress fractures do not show up on X-rays until the bone healing process gets under way and the new bone growth begins to show. Without more elaborate examination procedures, it is difficult to assess a stress fracture with accuracy and suspicion of such should lead to a referral to the patient's GP who can decide the next move.

Deep massage, effleurage and petrissage of the calf area should begin immediately and massage to the anterior muscles after the first two days. This should become increasingly deeper to cleanse and flush away the accumulated toxic wastes that will have built up in the muscles.

Stretching exercises for the calf muscles, the antagonistic group, may be started early in the treatment and, after the acute stage of the injury is over, isometric exercises of the dorsiflexors should commence, gradually increasing in intensity provided there are no adverse symptoms.

'Shin splints' must always be examined and treated with great care. The patient must be referred to a GP or podiatrist for more expert examination and treatment if there are any unusual symptoms or if there is failure to respond reasonably to treatment. Teachers should take note of dancers complaining of shin pain and keep a careful watch over their activities to prevent the condition worsening.

Stress Fractures

It is not unusual for dancers to suffer from stress fractures of bones. The most common sites being the long bones of the foot, the metatarsals and the long bones of the lower leg, tibia and fibula.

They can occur in anyone from about the age of seven upwards. They usually occur as the result of prolonged and/or repeated loading on the legs, e.g. more intense dance sessions than the dancer is used to doing or to dancers who are not as well conditioned as they should be. This latter incidence may happen after a lay-off due to injury or ill-health or even a long but inactive holiday.

The most common sites are the heel bone, the navicular and the metatarsals with the second metatarsal the most commonly occurring one in ballet dancers.

The symptoms are of pain in a specific bone during dancing with a distinct tenderness on palpation of the bone. There may be some discernible local swelling. The discomfort becomes worse and the dancer may not be able to take his or her weight on the injured foot. The injury will not show on X-ray until the new bone growth of healing is evident.

► Figure 4.2:
    The foot.

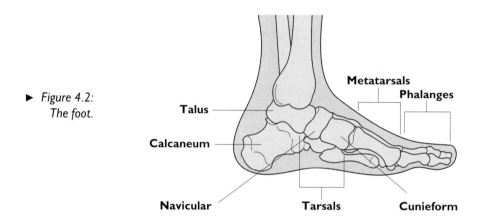

The main thrust of treatment is to rest from any activities that cause the painful symptoms. The dancer should not try and dance through the pain with any injury but should request medical examination. Massage above the site of the stress fracture will help drainage away from the site of the injury and exercises for the injured and uninjured legs to maintain tone and flexibility should be included from the earliest treatments.

Prevention of a re-occurrence should take into account a re-assessment of training and competition schedules and an examination of footwear or any equipment that may have a bearing upon the onset of the injury.

Hallux Valgus

Hallux valgus, known also as a bunion, is one of the most common and painful conditions of the foot and may occur to just about anyone, dancer or not.

It is a deviation of the big toes in its alignment to the smaller toes and happens over a period of time. Thus, it is a progressive condition in which the fluid in the bursa at the first metatarso-phalangeal joint becomes inflamed and results in what is commonly termed a 'bunion'. Additionally, discomfort is brought about by the appearance of a corn that forms in the centre of the bunion and the pain can be, on occasions, excruciating.

Hallux valgus is caused by the failure of the muscles that act to keep the big toes in line (flexor hallucis longus and brevis, extensor hallucis longus and brevis and adductor hallucis). Balanced muscles will keep the toe in alignment and, if no other factors are involved, the toe will remain in line. If something or some activity causes the adductor hallucis tendon to weaken and lengthen and the other muscles tighten and shorten, the big toe will be forced towards the smaller one and the condition of hallux valgus begins. Care should be taken with young dancers that their muscles are not put under pressures with which they cannot cope.

As the big toe deviates, the metatarsal splays outwards to form the medial projection that is so characteristic of this condition. Pressure of footwear against this projection will produce in turn; tenderness, inflammation, callus formation, adventitous bursa, corn and bunion.

Possible causes include narrow fitting shoes, especially with pointed toes; tight stockings pointed at the centre rather than shaped to the foot; a '10 to 2' position of the feet when walking; hereditary.

Treatment for Hallux Valgus

Chronic, severe cases may only be successfully helped by surgery, due to the onset of osteoarthritis in the joint in addition to the build up of fibrous tissue and chronic inflammation.

Caught in the early stages, the affected dancer should be referred to a podiatrist but the therapist may also offer treatment, too. This would consist of foot massage, a valgus strapping and ultrasound or interferential treatment twice a week. The massage should be quite deep and include passive flexion and extension movements of the toe. Footwear should be thoroughly checked. If the corn has appeared, the patient should be referred to the podiatrist for treatment.

Massage treatments are important parts of most treatment plans, especially those involving feet. Spilken (1990) recommended massage for conditions like tired feet, stress and in other injuries and conditions of the dancer's foot.

Hallux Rigidus

This is a condition in which the first metatarso-phalangeal joint will neither dorsi nor plantar flex; the big toe has stiffened and will not bend. This is usually caused by a traumatic incident such as forcibly stubbing the toe against something solid. Occasionally, this condition may be the result of having something dropped on the foot causing bleeding and bruising in and around the joint. In the non-traumatic condition, hallux rigidus may be associated with another foot problem like pes planus that may impose a severe strain upon the joint and the onset of osteoarthritis.

The patient begins to experience problems in simple everyday walking. Because there is no dorsiflexion in the joint, the push-off phase may mean that the individual walks onto the tip of his or her toes or the foot may be moved to compensate and the inner side of the toe is used to push-off.

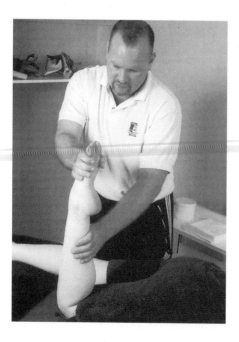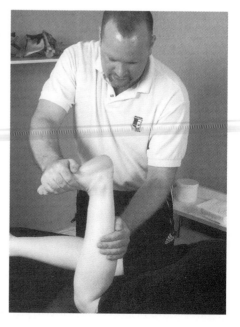

▲ *Figure 4.3:*
(a) Plantar flexion, and; (b) dorsiflexion of the foot.

Upon examination, there is usually a little passive plantar flexion possible and this may well be the key to initiating treatment. If there is no movement and the joint is completely rigid, the patient should be referred, possibly to an orthopaedic surgeon.

If there is evidence of movement, treatment by massage of the foot is indicated. Included in this treatment will be frictions around the affected joint and passive movements of both plantar and dorsiflexion. A simple but very controlled traction movement will be beneficial and both ultrasound and faradic treatment should be added. Sometimes this condition responds very quickly to massage treatment and only three or so treatments are required to restore good movement to the joint.

Pain in the Foot (Metatarsalgia)

Pain in the metatarsal area, i.e. the joints where the long bones of the foot meet the toes, is a very common condition and occurs amongst dancers, too. It can hurt severely and is often described by sufferers as a deep burning pain.

The anterior heads of the metatarsals form the anterior metatarsal arch of the foot. The metatarsal heads at the base of the big toe and the little toe, along with the heel bone, are important weight bearing points; the metatarsal heads 2, 3 and 4 are raised and form the arch. Unfortunately, in some individuals, the metarsals drop and begin to take an undue share of the body's weight.

The effect is that the pressure on the metatarsal heads produces pain and may cause a painful neurological reaction, especially the nerves that run between the metatarsal bones.

On examination of the affected foot, the therapist will find that the plantar surface of the foot will actually bulge in the area of the arch instead of slightly arching. Palpation of the metatarsal heads will produce pain and there will likely be a callus formation under the affected joints. The smaller toes may tend to become plantar flexed and develop corns over the proximal metatarso-phalangeal joints. In long-term cases, periostitis may develop in the shafts of the metatarsals near the anterior heads and there could be traumatic arthritis of the metatarso-phalangeal joints.

Among the causes of this condition, the following are believed to play a part, either singly or in combination:

- The weakening of supportive muscles due to long-term illness;
- Straining of the muscles due to a sudden increase in weight;
- Muscle strain caused by changes in working habits,
  e.g. standing too long;
- Wearing of high-heeled shoes.

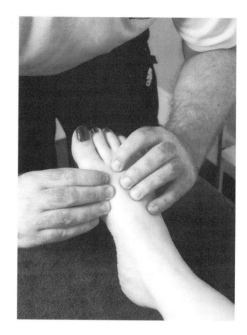

▶ *Figure 4.4:*
Shaking of the metatarsals.

Treatment of Metatarsalgia

The first consideration in the treatment of metatarsalgia is the relief of pain. If there are corns present, send the patient to a chiropodist for this aspect of the treatment.

Massage the foot and ankle and then pad and strap the three inner metatarsal heads to help guide the bones of the arch into its correct position. The patient should wear this pad and strapping for 8–10 days but returning to the therapist for changing and re-padding as necessary.

After this period, there should be further massage to the foot, with the aim of breaking down adhesions, reducing swelling, restoring flexibility and stimulating the circulation. This massage treatment should include deep frictions around the metatarsal heads and mobilising (commonly called 'shaking') of the bones and joints. A faradic foot bath with a fairly strong current applied for 10–15 minutes will also help in this treatment. The pad should then be replaced and strapped into position for a further 8–10 days. When the patient returns at the end of this stage of treatment, the pad and strapping may be removed permanently and the patient receives three further deep massage and faradic treatments in the next 7–8 days. In many cases, there will be a dramatic improvement, but each patient will have to be re-assessed and the treatment plan modified in each case according to the patient's needs.

Blisters and Other Conditions

Blisters occur due to friction, usually within the skin, a fluid accumulation within the layers. For this to happen, the surface of the skin must momentarily stick to the material with which it is in direct contact, i.e. the shoe, sock, even adhesive tape. Socks are worn to provide a smooth interface between footwear and skin to avoid sticking and friction. Socks allow friction to take place where it does no harm, between sock and shoe. Thus the sock becomes an extension of the shoe.

The first stage is identified as a local hot spot, tender and red. At this stage, the blister can be treated by a doughnut pad or covered with *Second Skin*. Once the inter-dermal tissue is exposed to friction or pressure, it becomes painful and a blister forms. This can become painful and limits movement and may become infected which can mean time away from dancing.

Little blisters should be left to heal by themselves. Larger blisters should be drained under sterile conditions. The therapist must wear protective gloves if draining the blister. A puncture is made at the edge of the blister and the fluid allowed to drain. The covering layer of skin must be retained as intact as possible. If the blister has already broken, it should be treated for infection and the covering skin smoothed out as far as possible. Then cover the blister with *Second Skin* and add a smear of *Vaseline* to prevent any further friction.

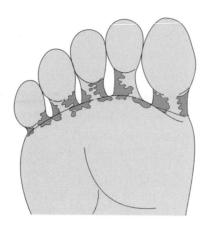

◀ *Figure 4.5:*
Athlete's foot.

Prevention of blisters should be a priority. Make sure that socks are free from holes, clean, dry and the correct fit. Similarly, shoes must be suitable for the job for which the dancer is using them; they must be the correct size and fit. Meticulous foot hygiene must always be observed.

Athlete's Foot

As has already been mentioned, dancers and therapists find it frustrating when an unavoidable injury stops the dancer from performing. We have also mentioned the importance of correct equipment, especially well fitting shoes. If this is not the case, it is very easy for a dancer to pick up blisters that will stop them from performing.

Athlete's foot is often picked up in humid damp areas, such as changing rooms. It is a fungal infection that can cause irritation, discomfort and in the worst cases, could lead to a dancer not being able to perform to the best of their potential. It can be avoided by thorough washing and drying of feet, and applying talcum powder. It is not a good idea to share a towel either. If this advice is followed, the dancer has less chance of being susceptible to this common condition.

Verrucas

These nasty afflictions can cause considerable discomfort and interfere with dance activities. They originate from virus infections transferred from one person to another via floors to bare feet. There is a lengthy incubation period of up to six months and, sometimes, difficult to trace back to the source of infection. Always wear some form of footwear in places used by other people and the public and, as mentioned above, observe meticulous foot hygiene.

Verrucas can be very painful, especially when they are on weight bearing joints or with calluses. Treat by bathing the foot in hot water for fifteen minutes. You may rub the verruca with an emery board and apply one of the proprietory brands of treatments available from your pharmacist until the condition heals. Prevention is the best treatment.

Nail Problems

If you have a nail problem consult a chiropodist/podiatrist quickly. Nail problems that are allowed to develop can become serious and prevent the dancer from dancing. Observe all the rules of foot hygiene. Trim toe nails on a weekly basis. Make sure that you always wear clean and suitable shoes and socks. Bacterial infections are very painful and disabling.

Blackened nails appear as the result of a blow, being trodden on, by allowing nails to grow too long or by wearing unsuitably narrow footwear. Bleeding occurs into the nail bed and appears black. It can cause pain due to the build up of pressure under the nail. Get professional treatment to drain and disinfect the nail and avoid further, painful problems that will seriously interfere with dancing.

Sometimes, nails become thickened and discoloured because of a fungoid infection. Again, the dancer must be totally hygienic in avoiding infection but, once it happens, make an appointment with the chiropodist for treatment and advice. Proprietary fungicides are available from a pharmacy but the dancer should seek expert treatment rather than opt for self-help for any conditions that may threaten the dancing career.

Chapter 5
Young Dancers and Injuries

Regular practise and dancing is of course, very common. Not only in dancing, but in many sports, participants begin at a very early age and may train for two hours and five or six days per week (Petersen and Renstrom, 1986). Examples are well-documented in sports like swimming, gymnastics and figure skating. It is difficult to predict whether the enthusiastic five-year old will become a future star at senior level but the over-riding principle at this age is that all sport (and that includes dancing) should be fun and not involve hard, even painful training.

Young people are spontaneously active (Caldwell, 1990) but by adolescence only about twenty-five per cent engage in vigorous activity – many become lazy and obese as they adapt to a Westernised adult lifestyle. At any age, the benefits of dancing and exercise should be balanced against the risks involved.

This is a survey of some of the conditions, both general and specific, that may happen to dancers from starting their careers right through their teenage years. Teachers, parents and therapists should be on the lookout for any condition that causes pain and tends to become worse rather than better in just a few days. Fairclough (1992) succinctly put it that, "No child should limp." It is a good standpoint; a child who develops a painful limp must be examined and given the best possible treatment as quickly as possible.

Children are not miniature adults, rather they are in the process of growing. Thus, they do not tolerate the same volume of activity as grown-ups. Children are vulnerable, physically and also emotionally, psychologically and socially. Adults are sometimes guilty of what Briggs (2000) described as the 'abuse' of children because of the stresses to which they subject those in their charge.

- Overuse/overtraining/overdancing (Sperryn, 1983) should be avoided.
- Risks to musculoskeletal system (Petersen and Renstrom, 1986).
- Injuries due to trauma, especially amongst adolescents (Lachman, 1988).
- Injuries to growth zone epiphysis. An injury to such an area can adversely affect growth in that area whilst other areas continue to grow normally. Overtraining or practising may cause this type of injury.
- *Perthe's Hip.* A rare condition in which the head of the femur fragments and becomes compressed. It is painful and any young dancer who develops a painful limp should be investigated and referred to their GP.
- *Slipped Upper Femoral Epiphysis.* Another condition in which the hip is affected. The child suffers pain and develops a limp and the therapist should investigate quickly and refer the child to his or her doctor for further examination.
- *Osgood-Schlatter's Syndrome.* This condition is quite common in enthusiastic dancers and athletes. It is a condition affecting the insertion of the quadriceps muscle into the tibia at the tibial tubercle below the knee joint; epiphysitis (inflammation of the epiphysis) of the tibial tubercle. Symptoms include aching which may develop into pain, heat and swelling with a possible distortion of the bone in extreme cases and avulsion (separation). Any dancer who complains of knee pain must be thoroughly investigated and referred to a doctor. This condition is serious and may bring about an early finish to a promising career. It does respond well to treatment by rest and massage but it may take many weeks and even months for the dancer to recover well enough to resume dancing.
- *Osteochondritis Dissecans.* This tends to occur in the early to mid teens and is a fragmentation of bone and or cartilage into the knee joint. It produces locking of the knee, swelling and pain. It is potentially serious and may require surgery.
- *Calcaneal Epiphysitis.* This refers to a stress factor of the growth plate of the heel bone that in children has not united with the main

body of the bone. The cause is usually an overuse problem from the musculo-tendinous stress via the Achilles tendon and its insertion into the calcaneum. This will require rest, support, exercises for the leg muscles and exercise/dancing on soft surfaces for some time until recovery is complete. Heel pain (and any persisting foot pain) must be taken seriously, investigated and probably referred to the child's GP who will request further examination, probably including an X-ray that will confirm the condition.

The therapist may treat the dancer with this condition but only after examination by a doctor. The treatment involves rest from strenuous or painful activities. A heel pad cut out from thin chiropody felt and worn under the painful heel is beneficial in relieving pressure and discomfort. The therapist should massage the foot and the calf muscles three times a week until the condition improves and daily applications of an anti-inflammatory gel or ointment will also help the condition to improve in the acute stage.

Chapter 6
Knee Injuries

Structure of the Knee Joint

The knee is involved in a wider variety and a larger number of injuries than any other area of the body. This is especially true of dancers and sports people. Its complex and crucial mechanism is subject to very many injuries (Macnichol 1998), the diagnosis of which and, thus, the treatments are often less than straightforward. The knee is highly susceptible to both direct and indirect injuries.

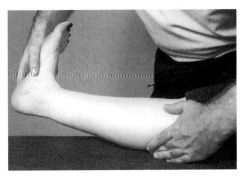

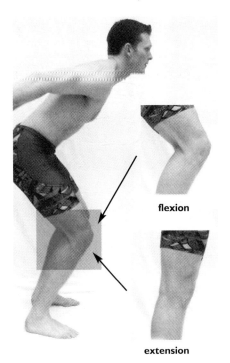

flexion

extension

◄▲ *Figure 6.1:*
Ranges of movement of the knee –
extension and flexion.
Photograph showing the raised heel,
pointing towards 'hyper-' extension
of the knee.

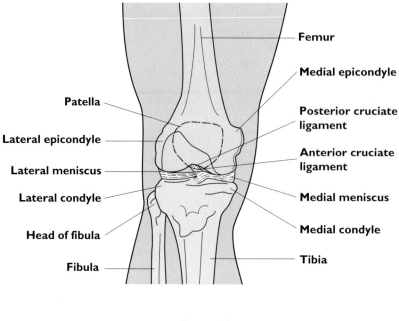

▲ *Figure 6.2:*
The knee joint.

The knee is the largest joint in the body. It is a hinged joint and the main movements are flexion and extension but with some rotation possible when in the flexed position. The articular bodies of the knee joint consist of the femoral condyles, the tibial condyles and the patella. It is also an incongruent joint, i.e. its articulations do not fit snugly into place like pieces of a jigsaw. The incongruence is compensated, by a relatively thick cartilaginous covering by the menisci and the synovial fluid.

The patella or kneecap is a sesamoid bone of a roughly triangular shape. The upper third of the patella serves as part of the attachment of the quadriceps tendon and the lower third serves as the origin for the patellar ligament that inserts into the tibial tubercle. Occasionally the therapist will encounter variants, for example, patellar bipartita in which the bone feels and appears to be in two distinct parts or sections and patellar emarginata in which the lateral edge appears to be absent.

The femur is the longest bone in the body and articulates with the hipbone as well as forming an integral part of the knee joint.

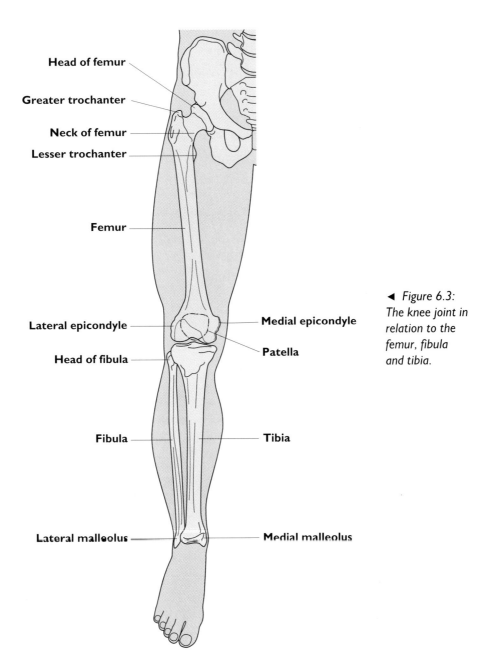

Head of femur

Greater trochanter

Neck of femur

Lesser trochanter

Femur

Lateral epicondyle

Head of fibula

Fibula

Lateral malleolus

Medial epicondyle

Patella

Tibia

Medial malleolus

◄ *Figure 6.3:*
The knee joint in
relation to the
femur, fibula
and tibia.

The tibia lies under the femur and is protected by, among others, the menisci and the tough articulating cartilages. The fibula plays a more minor part in knee function. It corresponds approximately in length with the tibia but is a slimmer and more flexible bone. The two bones are connected at both the proximal and distal ends and by the tense, fibrous interosseus membrane.

The major muscles of the knee joint are the quadriceps which bring about extension or straightening and the hamstrings which flex or bend the knee. The small amount of rotation that is possible when the knee is already flexed involves, in addition to the hamstrings, a contribution from gracilis, sartorius and popliteus.

Synovia

Synovium is a mesothelium, one of the tissues that line the body like periosteum, pericardium and pleura. It is made up of two layers:

1. A thin layer of cells called the serous layer, and;
2. The underlying fibrous layer. The synovial fluid comes from this layer.

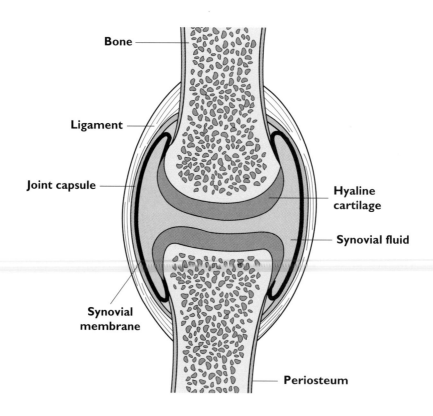

▲ *Figure 6.4:*
Synovial joint.

The synovium lines the inside of the fibrous capsule of the joint but is separated from it by fatty deposits and is attached to each bone at the edge of the articular cartilage. The synovium does not cover the weight bearing surfaces of the knee joint and is not found on the articular cartilages or the menisci.

Synovial fluid provides lubrication at the joint. The fluid is secreted at the periphery of the joint and is swept across the joint by movement and the villi (tiny hair-like projections) deliver the fluid deeply between the surfaces. The fluid also contains the nutrition for the articulating cartilage. Care of the knee joint requires regular movement that will stimulate the secretion of the fluid so necessary to its wellbeing.

Upon injury to the knee joint, the synovial fluid takes part in the general inflammatory reaction and the joint is flooded (effused) with fluid as a protective measure. The fluid now loses its lubricating and nutritional attributes and exercising or dancing on an effused knee joint has potential for further damage. Such swelling can cause pain due to pressure and also due to irritation that may be caused to nerve endings. On occasions an injured knee may swell very quickly and this is a sign that there has been an effusion of blood into the joint. This must be seen and treated by a doctor without delay.

There are a number of bursae around the knee joint. They are fluid filled sacs that are positioned to prevent friction that may arise when soft tissues, for example, tendons, come into contact with harder tissues, for example, bones, during movement. Occasionally, these may react to pressure and become swollen, even inflamed, and show as fairly hard, distinct bumps just under the surface of the skin around the joint.

Osgood-Schlatter's Syndrome

This is a painful knee condition that may affect teenage dancers. The symptoms include:

*   Pain just below the knee joint at the tibial tubercle;
*   Swelling around the tubercle;
*   Dancing makes it more painful, as do running and jumping;
*   Squatting is difficult and painful;
*   Knee flexion is limited.

The injury occurs at the attachment of the strong quadriceps muscles into the tibia. It occurs usually in active teenagers (although the onset may occur in younger children). The strength of the muscle groups and the frequent use of the muscles combine to damage the attachment of the muscle at the bone. It is progressively painful, becomes inflamed and sensitive to touch and will not get better until the causes of the condition are investigated and dealt with.

If the dancer displays these symptoms, the therapist must ensure that the dancer's GP is informed and examines the knee. It may be serious enough to require referral to a paediatric orthopaedic consultant, or it may be serious enough, if not spotted and treated appropriately, to end a dancer's career.

Treatment (after examination by a doctor and with the doctors' approval) consists of:

- Rest from activity that aggravates the condition. In some cases, the child may be immobilised for a period of time in hospital;
- Anti-inflammatory measures including ice and a topical application such as *Enzyme Ice, Movelat* or homoeopathic *Ruta Grav* ointment;
- Effleurage and petrissage to the quadriceps and hamstrings to relax and cleanse the muscles which, in most cases, feel tight and hard;
- Commence gentle stretching exercises, especially for the quadriceps;
- When pain-free, strengthening exercises which may commence with isometric exercises and graduate to active and resisted exercises.

Treatments should be 2–3 times per week and the condition may persist for some months. The patient should not be put under pressure to resume dancing activities by peers, parents, teachers and the therapist should liaise with these key people and explain the condition and the treatment as fully as possible. Otherwise, the patient will not recover either as quickly or as completely.

Chronic Knee Pain

This condition is the long-term 'bad knee' with a long history experienced among older dancers. The probable cause is a succession of minor traumas over the years that have not healed properly and there may be adhesions at the joint, relics of previous injuries. On examination, no obvious derangement of the structures are revealed but the dancer reports aches and pains during and after dancing. Treatment for chronic knee pain includes effleurage and petrissage of the whole leg to ease and relax the muscles, to stimulate the circulation and to help clear out waste products.

With the patient supine on the table, flex and extend the knee several times and then take rapidly into full flexion. There may be an audible but pain-free cracking sound on the full flexion.

Place the patient's ankle on the therapist's shoulder and the therapist's hand is placed over the front of the knee joint. In one steady movement the therapist pulls the leg into full extension. Now the therapist stands facing the injured knee at the side of the patient. He puts the knee into flexion and holds the patient's thigh against his own body. The therapist's lower hand grasps the patient's ankle and rotates the patient's tibia in each direction.

After completing these movements, the therapist resumes with effleurage and petrissage to the whole leg, and frictions around the knee joint itself. Other options that will benefit the patient include faradic muscle stimulation and ultrasound. The dancer may need to do more stretching before and after dancing and there may be a need to formulate a training plan to strengthen the muscles.

Patello-femoral Problems

Persistent pain may occur around the kneecap. It may be caused by a weakness in one of the muscles, vastus medialis, for instance when returning to dancing after a lay-off due to illness or injury. Sometimes it is an overuse injury following unaccustomed or unusual intensity of dancing and practise. Dancing on hard surfaces predisposes some individuals to this injury. The patient may have some abnormality or biomechanical problem and this should be examined by a podiatrist.

The pain is often antero-medial but may be in other sites, for example, the superior border of the patella or even into the quadriceps insertion tendon. The patient reports that it hurts when ascending and descending stairs, squatting, weight bearing on a semi-flexed knee and after sitting down for longish periods. The condition eases on rest. On closer examination there is often evidence of weakness in vastus medialis, tenderness around the joint on palpation, possibly pain and tenderness in rectus femoris which may also feel tight and stiff. There may be swelling, some redness and heat on palpation.

The leg should be treated by both effleurage and petrissage. Pulsed ultrasound at 0.5 for four minutes. Ice may be applied for twenty minutes 2–3 times a day between the first treatment and the second treatment which should take place 2–3 days later. *Lasonil, Enzyme Ice* or any other suitable anti-inflammatory gel or cream should also be applied in the acute stage. Gentle stretching should begin early in the treatment. Once the pain subsides, the therapist may look at active and resisted exercises, where appropriate, to strengthen vastus medialis.

Impingement Syndrome

An impingement is the prevention of normal movement at the knee by some form of mechanical block, for example, a meniscus fragment or loose body, usually of bone. It may be a momentary block in which movement is temporarily blocked and accompanied by some discomfort or pain. It may be of a more prolonged nature and the knee is locked for some time, for example when caused by a bucket handle tear of the medial meniscus. Whatever the cause or nature of the impingement, it should be fully investigated medically before any treatment by the therapist.

One type of impingement causes a stab of pain in the knee when going up and down stairs. It is a brief stab and then tends to get more painful and quite frequent. There are no other diagnostic signs for the therapist to ponder. This is caused by a portion of the fatty pad, the pad of alar, getting between the bone ends of the joint and preventing full extension of the leg. It becomes inflamed and sets up frequent sharp stabs of pain.

This is treated by a heel pad of 3mm chiropody felt under the heel of the affected side. Interferential or pulsed ultrasound at 0.25 for three minutes graduating to five minutes three times in a week helps to improve the condition.

Examination of the Dancer's Knee

Plenty of time should be allowed in which to examine the injured knee. Listen to the patient's own account of the injury, and always ask about previous injuries and, indeed, the patient's past medical history. Careful examination is most important because without it, treatment will be ineffective.

Examine both the injured and the healthy knee by palpation, visually and by movements. Ask the patient to point to where the pain is; it saves time. Swelling is a sign of irritation, like a foreign body in an eye, and a good indicator of pathological damage.

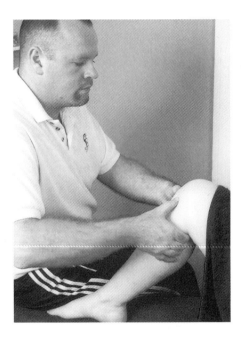

◄ *Figure 6.5:*
Examination of the knee.

A new click or noise may well be a loose body in the joint. Any noises or clicks must be taken into account and the patient must be questioned specifically about any noises that occurred at the time of the injury. Vague symptoms around the knee are often referred from hip or ankle and thus the examination of the patient may have to be extended to these joints. Laxity in the injured joint may indicate serious ligament injury.

Considerations for Treatment

The emphasis of knee care and knee treatment should always concentrate upon strengthening the muscles that work upon the knee. Strengthened muscles may be able to support the function of other injured tissue.

Muscle injuries around the knee will usually heal in 3–4 weeks. It is important to give the injury time to heal and not be in a rush to get back dancing. During this period, the muscles may have also weakened due to inactivity. The return to dancing after injury should be gradual. Do not go from complete inactivity one day to a full practise session the next. Resume with longer pre-dance warm up activities including stretching of the injured muscle. After the session, go through the warming down activities.

Meniscus Injury

The meniscus helps with load bearing, stability and lubrication of the knee joint. The medial meniscus is thicker and bigger than the lateral meniscus. It is subjected to a lot of pressure and strain and is susceptible to injury.

The meniscus is injured by traction forces on the knee, by compressive forces and by torque forces or all three in combination. The result is painful and often accompanied by swelling. It will be tender on palpation along the joint lines. Locking of the joint may occur but which may then suddenly release. Buckling or giving way is common with some injuries and a clicking noise may become apparent. The muscles of the quadriceps begin to atrophy within days.

Meniscus injuries always require first class medical examination and treatment. The medial meniscus is much more likely to suffer injury than the lateral meniscus. Get expert medical help as quickly as possible to prevent further damage. Years ago, meniscus injury could finish a dancer's career. Now, techniques are so good that it may only mean 8–10 days before the dancer can practise again. Massage treatment will be very helpful after surgery.

Ligament Injury

Ligament injuries, particularly to the collatoral and cruciate ligaments, are more serious in many cases. They are painful and the joint becomes unstable. They take months to heal with good treatment and, again, the healing process should not be rushed or cut short. However, with good care, most ligament injuries will heal and the dancer can resume dancing. Massage treatment with frictions will be most helpful right from the acute stage of the injury to eventual return to dancing.

Patella Subluxation

Patella subluxation, which is de-alignment or dislocation of the knee joint, tend to be recurrent and the patient usually has a record of previous episodes. The patient should undergo a full medical investigation, after which massage treatment may be helpful during the recovery period.

Chapter 7
Hip Injuries

Structure of the Hip Joint

The hipbones consist of three parts; the pubis, the ilium and the ischium. They join together at the front at the symphysis pubis, and at the back, the ilia articulate with the sacrum. The joint formed between the head of the femur and the acetabulum is the most movable joint of the hip complex and the one that is of most concern to the dancer and the therapist.

There are five ligaments that stabilise the joint between head of femur and acetabulum and allow movements of flexion, extension, abduction, adduction, lateral and medial rotation and circumduction; a very mobile joint when compared to its neighbour, the knee joint. Movement is brought about by combinations of muscles, some of which will be discussed in greater detail later in this section of the book. Nerve supply to the hip region is from both the lumbar and a sacral plexi and includes the largest nerve in the body, the sciatic nerve.

Examination of the Dancer's Hip

Hip pain may be symptomatic of a hip injury or it may be referred pain from a low back injury. Cyriax (1974) stated that hip pain was generally the result of osteoarthritis or lumbar disc injury and that most buttock pain has a lumbar origin. However, injuries to muscles, for example, piriformis, must also be taken into consideration. Buttock pain may also be caused by ischial bursitis, injury to hamstring origin or the proximal hamstring or possibly an ovarian cyst. Very careful and thorough examination is required.

The normal examination procedure should be adhered to and include the patient's subjective account of the injury (Apley and Solomon, 1997), examination by palpation, visual examination and examination by movement. Visual examination would include observation of the patient walking or dancing as well as a more static visual examination on the

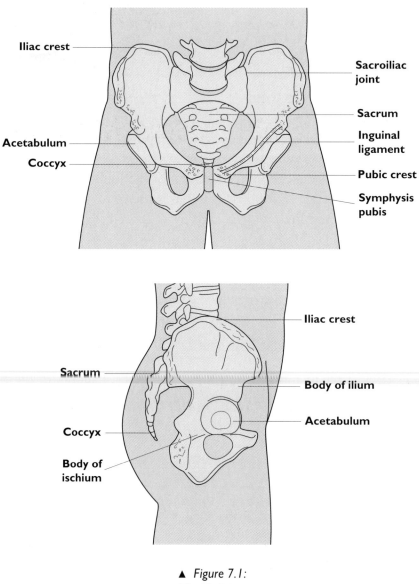

▲ Figure 7.1:
The hip joint.

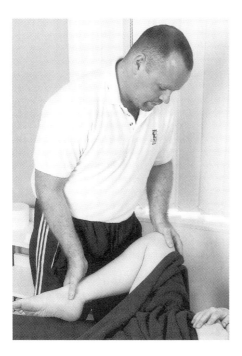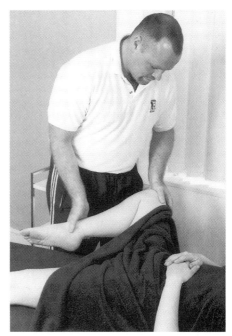

▲ *Figure 7.2a and b:*
Circumduction of the hip.

treatment table. Any other evidence, for example the results of any X-ray, should also be taken into consideration.

Examination With the Patient Lying on Their Back on the Table

- Check that the legs and pelvis are positioned square with the table.
- Check and see if the patient has an excessive lumbar lordosis in this position; it may indicate a fixed flexion at the hips.
- Can the patient flex one hip and does the other hip also lift off the table? Again, this may indicate a problem with flexion.
- Check the anterior iliac spines and the greater trochanters of the femurs for balance.

Examine the length of each leg and note any discrepancy. This may be done initially by the therapist by comparing the relative positions of the malleoli. This will give a good indication of equal length or otherwise. If there is a leg length difference, the therapist must find the cause for it and it may be necessary to refer the patient to a podiatrist.

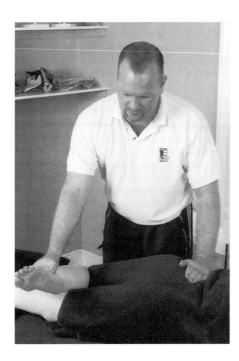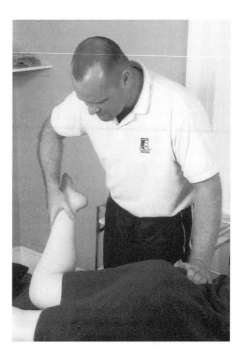

▲ Figure 7.3:
(a) External, and; (b) internal hip rotation.

Two Hip Disorders in Young Dancers

There are two conditions that may affect younger dancers with which all those concerned with dancers and dancing should be familiar. The first of these, Perthe's Hip, occurs in younger dancers in the age range 5–10 years. It is an avascular necrosis of the head of the femur and requires immediate medical attention. The head of the femur is deprived of its blood supply and the bone begins to die. The second condition, Slipped Upper Femoral Epiphysis, affects older children and teenagers. In this condition, the new bone growth is unable to cope with the demands of weight bearing and begins to disintegrate.

Both conditions are of quite sudden onset with the child complaining at first, of pain after dancing. The pain becomes more generalised, dancing becomes impossible and the child develops a pronounced limp. The patient must be referred for a thorough medical examination as quickly as possible.

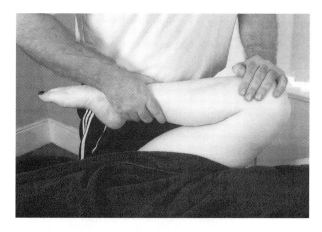

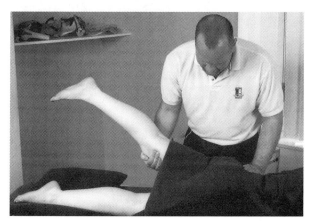

◄ *Figure 7.4:*
(a) Flexion, and;
(b) extension of the hip.

Clicking at the Hip

Clicking noises, especially without accompanying discomfort or pain, are nothing to worry about. The noise may be caused by the ilio-femoral ligament moving across the head of the femur or the iliotibial band (ITB) sliding back and to over the greater trochanter of the femur. This may disappear after massage to the hip muscles and some stretching exercises particularly to tensor fasciae latae.

Osteoarthritis of the Hip

This painful condition may develop as the result of excessive wear and tear of the joint or as the result of a previous injury. There are a number of possible causative factors. Osteoarthritis is usually of long, slow onset and may not show signs until middle – or even old age. Occasionally it becomes evident in younger people. On X-ray investigation, early signs of

▶ *Figure 7.5:*
Lordosis seen from
a standing position.

osteoarthritis may be seen in people under the age of twenty. This is not to say that the person concerned will be immediately affected by pain, stiffness, loss of movement or even deformity. The early signs may be present but the effects of the disease may not manifest themselves until much later in life.

In those who do develop osteoarthritis of the hip, pain in the groin is felt typically after activity and may radiate towards the knee. Later it becomes more constant and interrupts sleep. The joint feels stiff, a limp develops and the leg feels shorter. Osteoarthritis of the hip or other joints can be helped by massage and movement and may become so severe that surgery is inevitable.

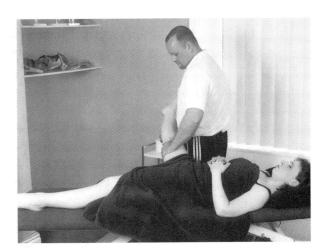

► *Figure 7.6:*
Abduction of the hip.

Hip Injuries and Dancers

Symptoms of a hip injury may be vague and non-specific and pain may spread towards the groin area. Pain and inflammation may be the result of over-exertion and over-loading muscles and their attachments into the bones. Frequently injured muscles in dancers include the adductors, iliopsoas, quadriceps and hamstrings.

Adductors

Adductor longus is vulnerable to injury. It arises from the pubic bone and inserts into the mid-shaft of the femur. It may be injured by a side kick or during intense work, especially on hard, unforgiving surfaces. Pain and tenderness is often felt at the origin and the pain may radiate into the groin. The worse the injury, the more painful it will prove and the dancer will be unable to contract the muscle and to actively adduct the hip.

Iliopsoas

This is a strong flexor of the hips and attaches to the lesser trochanter and to the ilium and spinal vertebrae as far as the ribs. When injured there may be pain in the groin on active flexion of the hips and there may be a knock-on effect to the lumbar spine.

Pain in the groin area may also be associated with rectus femoris injury and rectus abdominis injury. The male groin is particularly susceptible to injury and as well as the muscular injuries referred to, there may also be injuries associated with the external oblique aponeurosis and the inguinal ligament.

Pain in the centre of the pubic bone may be symptomatic of an injury to the symphysis pubis. Milder incidences will recover with rest from aggravating activities. More serious cases will take several months to heal and some will require the intervention of the surgeon.

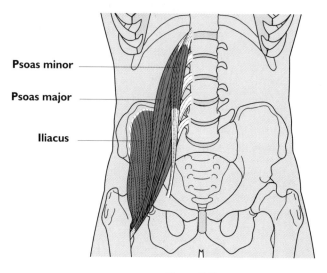

Psoas minor

Psoas major

Iliacus

▲ *Figure 7.7:*
The iliopsoas muscles.

Iliotibial Tract (ITT) or Band (ITB)

The ITT is a thickened band of deep fascia of the thigh extending from the tubercle of the iliac crest down the lateral aspect of the thigh to Gerdy's tubercle on the lateral tibial condyle. Occasionally it becomes irritated and may appear as lateral hip or lateral knee pain.

Tensor fasciae latae arise from the anterior iliac crest and superior anterior iliac spine and insert into the ITT. Fibres from gluteus maximus also insert into ITT which functions as a conjoin tendon of insertion for both muscles and permits them to act upon the knee joint as well as the hip joint. The distal ITT moves over the lateral femoral condyles as the knee is flexed and extended.

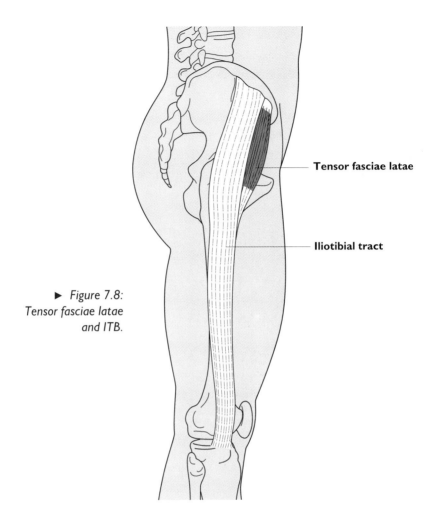

Tensor fasciae latae

Iliotibial tract

▶ *Figure 7.8:*
Tensor fasciae latae
and ITB.

Injury is usually caused by overuse; either excessive friction at the distal end or excessive tension at the proximal end. Excessive pronation or supination, leg length discrepancy, genu varum (bowlegged), cross-over gait, weakness in either or both the quadriceps and gluteals are all thought to be contributing factors to the injury. Examination may lead the therapist to refer the patient before planning treatment.

Piriformis

A common problem is that of piriformis spasm. Piriformis is a small muscle that lies under gluteus maximus. It originates on the anterior surface of the sacrum and inserts into the greater trochanter of the femur. Amongst its functions are involvement in extension, abduction and rotation of the hips. It helps in lateral directional changes when dancing and in curves and turns.

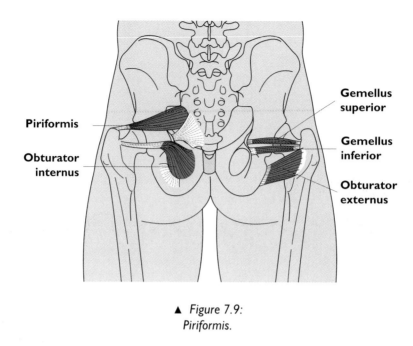

▲ *Figure 7.9:*
Piriformis.

Piriformis (and other gluteals) contract when the leg is extended in front and serve to give stability to the ball and socket joint.

Piriformis has a proximity to the sciatic nerve that passes through a foramen alongside the muscle. In rarer cases, the nerve (the common peroneal part of the sciatic nerve) passes through the piriformis itself. Changes in the shape and size of piriformis due to spasm or inflammation may result in pressure on the sciatic nerve, causing pain and weakness in the other gluteals and even into the leg muscles.

Piriformis spasm is treated by gluteal massage which includes deep crossfibre goading of the muscles, manual muscle belly pressure and stretching of the muscle. Preventative measures include daily flexibility training including stretching exercises.

Hip muscles respond to deep massage, including frictions at the origins and insertions, muscle belly pressure, passive movements performed by the therapist during the treatment and stretching and flexibility exercises performed by the dancer before and after dancing.

Chapter 8
Psychology and Dance

As a massage therapist, the fabric of my job is to deal with injuries and rehabilitation. In the eyes of the dancer, the therapist sorts out muscles, tendons and ligaments; nothing more, nothing less. In many senses, this is true. However, to do this to the best of their capabilities, the therapist has to be aware of several aspects before he begins to start the practical aspect of his or her work.

One important area is for the therapist to have the right personal qualities to gain the trust of the dancer, their parents and dance teacher/s. This is usually and hopefully done by the therapist being themselves. The therapist should be efficient and uncomplicated, but also approachable and humane. A dancer has to have complete confidence in their therapist. This does not happen if the therapist is cold and aloof or unfamiliar and unconcerned.

Initially, the therapist should let the dancer talk; sit them down and allow them to tell you everything about the injury, whether relevant or not. Dancers, along with many sports people are performers and become highly attached to their work. This can lead to them becoming highly emotional when describing their injuries to the therapist. From the therapist's point of view, he/she should not become confused or influenced by any show of emotion. It is often found with dancers and other sports people that trivial injuries are played up – "I'll never dance/perform/compete again" and that serious injuries are played down – "It's nothing serious." The important words for the therapist to adhere to during the initial examination and consultation stages of an injury are listen, look and palpate. Palpation is simply touching an injured area to ascertain how painful it is and to get a 'feel' for the injury.

Usually a dancer wants to know if they can carry on dancing or if they have to stop dancing, and the whole question of rest. Again the therapist has to be firm without being overpowering. Remember that injuries can be as stressful as auditions and performances – without the accompanying 'buzz' or 'high'.

Whilst being careful not to cover up the severity of an injury, the therapist should be able to point out any positives. Many dancers who become injured can use the rehabilitation time as a positive tool. In some cases, they can use the time to heal other, less serious, chronic injuries. Others will use the time to improve cardiovascular fitness or mobility, or catch up with academic studies. At the same time, their boundaries and goals of rehabilitation must be clarified.

During the traumatic period, many dancers will get depressed, to varying degrees. It is the responsibility of the therapist to keep them involved with the recovery; dancers will feel isolated from their peers, and less important than them in the eyes of the teacher. Whilst this is not always true, it is easy to see why dancers can imagine it happening.

It is not just dance where these scenarios are the case. Chris Peet, in his paper, *The Role of the Coach With the Injured Player*, 1996, talks of the "devastation and heartbreak" of injury and that coaches and physiotherapists should provide "reassurance" and "regular contact with players (dancers) and their families." This even goes as far as providing related magazines and videos to ease any boredom that may result from the lay-off. This may even lead to intrinsic motivation whereby the player/dancer comes back raring to go. This should also be curbed in the right manner.

The therapist should be able to get the best out of the dancer, where a relationship or bond can build up, where they trust each other implicitly. If the dancer is being held back, they understand why, and when the therapist is told how rehabilitation is developing, he should feel confident that the dancer is being accurate. Whilst no-one likes being injured, the dancer should see treatment sessions as the focal point of the recovery. It is the responsibility of the therapist to cause this to happen and therefore the dancer should look forward to attending the treatment sessions.

When a dancer goes to a therapist for the first time, they are going to be nervous as well as in pain. Again, it is the responsibility of the therapist to diffuse the situation and be in control but not too officious. A therapist will govern how a dancer reacts to them, and the beginning of the first session is when the groundwork of your future rapport is built!

As we have said, although the persona of the therapist is important, there are also other factors that are important too. Similar to persona is appearance. It goes without saying that cleanliness, tidiness and hygiene are of vital importance. However, dancers and sports people generally will look for reassurance in the therapist's dress, attitude and demeanour. It may be that dancers will identify or connect better with someone who comes across as 'sporty'. For example, a polo shirt, tracksuit trousers and training shoes are probably more functional and appropriate than trousers and a tunic or a suit. It will reassure the dancer that the therapist is approachable and that they are interested in the unique nature of dance and sports injuries.

The condition of the area where the therapist works is also an indicator of the value placed on his/her work. With the proliferation of purpose built arenas, such as the City of Manchester Stadium at Eastland, the future home of Manchester City Football Club, medical and rehabilitation areas are given the utmost importance. There will be big expanses of space with thousands spent on state of the art equipment. However, in this real world, improvisation is the name of the game. One may argue that all the therapist needs is an examination couch and a body to work on! It would be beneficial if more importance was placed on this area. Indeed, I know of a Premiership football club, who have spent as much money as any other club on players in the last six years, where the massage therapist can only find room to put up his couch in the shower! Dancers and sports people will only take therapists as seriously as the surroundings they are in.

Another important factor for a therapist is the support they receive from other staff at an establishment. I have found there are possibly four different levels that this can work on.

1. Dance teachers and other staff to embrace you into the social culture of a college establishment. This is important and will enable a therapist to find a foothold to establish his roles within the organisation.

2. It will be often the case that dancers will only visit a therapist when they are sent by a dance teacher. Therefore, it is vital that teachers know your role, thus it may be that formal or informal meetings are set up to discuss any dancers that may be injured.

3. A good advert for a therapist is when dancers see their teachers coming in for treatment. They will see that the teachers respect you and your work, and hopefully that will be passed onto the dancer. Finally,

4. It is important that other staff members do not undermine the decisions you make with regards to rehabilitation of dancers. By this, it is meant that if the therapist prescribes a weeks' rest, then this means a weeks' rest. The last thing a therapist and a dancer needs is for a dance teacher to exert pressure on them to dance whilst injured. This will compromise the integrity of the therapist, cause friction between the teacher and therapist, confusion between the dancer and therapist, and ultimately – and most importantly, put the dancer at risk of making an injury worse.

Therefore, as one can see, it is important for a therapist to fit in with the fabric of dance life. I was lucky at Merseyside Dance and Drama Centre. I was accepted, backed up, given support and the Principal, Miss Owen came for preventative treatment nearly every week.

Chapter 9
Ideal Provision

As a lecturer, I have to be aware that whilst students need to know the theory behind different situations, it is vitally important that people are made aware of the differing gaps between theory and practice.

When a dancer comes to see me in private practice for treatment to an injury, we can sit down together and map out a plan for rehabilitation. I can also do the same with my dancers at Merseyside Dance and Drama Centre. With my private patient, there is a high chance that our plan will be adhered to. In a college environment, the chances of this are drastically reduced. It can be said in both situations that there are avoidable and unavoidable reasons and excuses for a treatment plan not being adhered to. We can group these together and call them 'barriers to treatment'. The better the therapist, the easier the barriers will be to negotiate.

The barriers can be grouped in different areas, such as time constraints, financial considerations and attitudes of the people involved.

Time constraints can be placed on treatment plan by either the therapist or the dancer. Generally I find that the busiest people are the ones that are most flexible when it comes to appointment times – it seems that they are accustomed to 'juggling' their diaries. On the other hand, particularly in private practice, it is people with very few time commitments who want the same time every week or month for their appointment. Hand on heart, I have heard clients say to me, "I can't have an appointment on Thursday, because I'm getting my hair done..... on Friday!" It seems that people with few appointments like to spread them out! However, it can be said also that if people are in need of treatment, they will usually come whenever you can fit them into your diary.

Ideally, a dancer should have a therapist that is easily accessible and therefore not causing time to be a barrier against treatment. If an injury is not treated adequately in its early stages it can mean an unnecessarily long lay off.

Another barrier to treatment is possibly finance. This depends on the situation. Does the therapist receive payment from the college that the dancer attends? Does the college part subsidise the treatments, or does the therapist see dancers and charge them like he does any other patient? It can be difficult at times if a young dancer cannot afford to pay for treatments on a regular basis. But a therapist cannot undersell him or herself. Personally from my past experience, all parties were happy with the financial set-up at Merseyside Dance and Drama Centre. This area can be a dilemma, but at the same time a therapist should never undervalue their work.

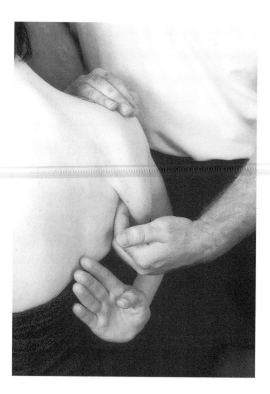

▶ *Figure 9.1:*
Scapula lift.

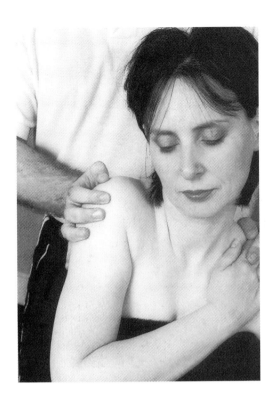

◄ *Figure 9.2:*
Shoulder circumduction.

▶ *Figure 9.3:*
Shoulder traction.

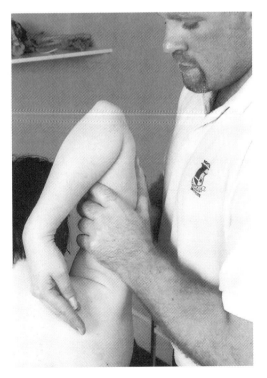

► *Figure 9.4:*
Hamstring stretch.

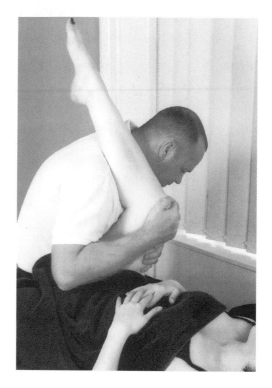

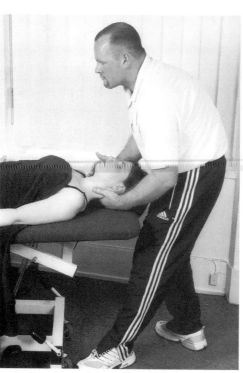

◄ *Figure 9.5:*
Neck traction.

◄ *Figure 9.6:*
Passive neck
movement.

It is also important that a barrier to recovery should not be due to the limitations of the therapist. What is not meant here is that every therapist should have an infinite amount of knowledge on every problem that can arise to every type of sports person. They should recognise that they have done all that can be done for a particular problem and then refer that person onto another medical professional. One example of this is passing onto a podiatrist, a dancer who needs an orthotic to correct a pronation problem. It will probably be that the therapist can cure the associated muscular and joint discomfort to knees, hips and backs, but until the initial problem is corrected, these secondary effects will persist. Therefore it is important that a therapist can identify primary and secondary symptoms, and if they are out of their sphere of expertise, then refer the dancer on. Thus, it is important that a therapist has a team of experts in allied areas that he can call upon.

A good model of this is the physiotherapy department at Manchester City F.C. The head physiotherapist, Rob Harris, has a specialist team of surgeons around the world who all deal in one particular area of the body. This is probably by no means unique, but is a model I am particularly aware of.

Whilst this area is vitally important, it should also be part of the therapist's job to ingratiate himself or herself in as many areas of injury and rehabilitation as is possible, especially in specialised areas, such as dance. It is not just the hands-on treatment in which a therapist has to be adept, but also in all manner of other areas of rehabilitation that the difference between an average therapist and a top notch therapist will be noticeable. As well as remedial treatments, the therapist should be able to use electrotherapy equipment, stretch bands and different types of mobilisation techniques, such as resisted movement, isometric movement, proprioceptive neuromuscular facilitation and passive movements.

All of these are vitally important at different times of rehabilitation from injury. It is also important that dancers hit the rehabilitation trail at exactly the right pace. There are all sorts of issues that need addressing here. How can a dancer work at basic cardiovascular fitness? Is swimming a good idea? In most situations, swimming is a good idea. It may be that a dancer is told not to do breast stroke with some groin injuries. Even if the injured dancer is only able to get in the water and 'splash around', it will help on both a physiological level and a psychological level. In many cases, an inactive, injured dancer leads to a frustrated, depressed dancer.

There are other areas that need consideration. How can muscle tone be kept at a high level when there is an associated joint injury? In this case, the answer is isometric stretching.

Ideally, a therapist should have an armoury that can deal with any dancer and their injury. From dealing with an acute injury from a first aid point of view, to looking after a chronic postural, overuse injury.

To do this, especially in a college environment, all barriers should be removed. The therapist should have plenty of time, space, knowledge and enthusiasm to spend with dancers that he/she is looking after.

The best situation for a dance college would be to have a full-time therapist who can then spend time on rehabilitation plans. There is nothing worse than working with dancers, and seeing injured dancers with no direction or plan, sitting glumly in the corner of a changing room or dance studio. A full-time therapist could take charge of a group of injured dancers, partly so that they do not feel alienated, but also to work with them on stretching, rehabilitation and education on prevention of injury.

In other full-time (professional) sports, a therapist may have up to half a dozen injured players at any one time. Because of their high level of base fitness, they can usually undertake rigorous rehabilitation programmes. I have seen injured premier league footballers turn up at the training ground at 7.45am, and still be there at 3.30pm, combining treatment, mobilisation and exercise. Obviously this is dependent on the nature of the injury. This same idea can be easily adapted to dancers and a dance college. This situation not only will make the therapist feel part of the college, but also enable the dancers and dance teachers to build up a good working relationship with the therapist.

To make the situation perfect, a dance college could have a small gymnasium area, where injured dancers can use cardiovascular equipment and light weights. This is an area that is very important and should not be neglected. Therefore, ideal provision knows no bounds. However, there are barriers that can and should be overcome to give dancers the best possible treatment and advice on injury, recovery and rehabilitation.

In the ever-changing dynamic world of dance, it is important to be as up-to-date as possible. One area where this is particularly important is the provision of treatment for dancers.

Over the summer of 2001, my colleagues at Merseyside Dance and Drama Centre were busy improving and expanding the facilities at their Camden Street headquarters. The treatment room has been expanded to include a Pilates studio.

This means that all students have extra room to stretch and warm up and down. However, where this is really advantageous is for the rehabilitation of injured dancers. In the past, if the dancers were sitting out a class, they were left in the corner of the room watching on forlornly. This new studio now means that the dancers who are injured can work as a little group with the therapist, doing any amount of rehabilitation work.

This will make the dancers feel more positive about their injury, and also give them more contact time with the therapist – also a positive benefit. This will lead to even more input from the therapist in educating dancers to minimise time spent off the dance floor and on the treatment table!

It can be said with great conviction that dance is a sport. It requires the grace of a synchronised swimmer, the strength of an athlete and the mobility of a gymnast. This is a truly unique combination that is reflected in dancers' injuries and their rehabilitation. The first skill of being a therapist within a niche area is to be endowed in the specificities of that specialisation.

For example, in athletics, is the injured athlete a hurdler or sprinter, a middle distance runner, hammer thrower or a long jumper? The same can be said of dancers; which kind of dance? How often do you dance?

It is an area of sport that is very challenging in its environment. There seems to be no lull in a dancer's year so anyone who is involved is never far away from pressure and deadlines – including the therapist. However, the special intrinsic value of seeing the pleasure that both the dancers and the audience get from a performance, make being their therapist all worthwhile.

Glossary of Terms

Acute
In remedial massage, this term is used for the early stages of an injury.

Agonist
A muscle or muscles responsible for joint movement, also known as prime mover.

Antagonist
The opposite of agonist (above). A muscle or group of muscles having the opposite action to the prime mover or agonist but which work with the agonist by relaxing muscle(s) and allowing movement to take place.

Articulation
Another word for a joint.

Atrophy
A decrease in the size of a tissue or organ, often caused in musculoskeletal structures by lack of use.

Attachments
Referred to also as the origins and insertions of muscles; where skeletal muscles are connected to bones.

Cartilage
Fibrous connective tissue, e.g. hyaline cartilage, elastic cartilage and fibrocartilage.

Chronic Pain
Pain that continues over a long period of time.

Concentric Contraction
The action of a prime mover where a muscle develops tension as it shortens in order to provide enough force to overcome resistance.

Cramp
A painful muscle spasm.

Eccentric Contraction
The muscle lengthens as it develops tension. The origin and insertion are pulled apart as the muscle resists and overcomes the movement/barrier.

Fibrocartilage   A connective tissue that permits little motion in joints and structures.

Inflammation   The protective response of the tissues to injury or irritation that may be acute or chronic.

Insertion   The distal attachment of a muscle.

Isometric Contraction   The action of the prime mover that occurs when tension develops within the muscle but no appreciable change occurs in the joint angle or length of the muscle. Movement does not occur.

Isotonic Contraction   The action of the prime mover that occurs when tension is developed in the muscle while it either shortens or lengthens.

Joint Capsule   The structure of connective tissue that connects the bony components of a joint.

Ligament   Connective tissue, mainly collagen, that connects bones and strengthens and stabilises joints.

Membrane   A thin elastic tissue covering the surface of certain organs and lining the cavities of the body.

Origin   The least movable attachment of a muscle; the proximal attachment.

Pes Cavus   A high arched foot.

Pes Planus   A flat foot in which the plantar arch has disappeared.

Pronation   Turning the palm of the hand downwards.

Referred Pain   Pain felt at some distance from its original site.

Sub-acute   A stage between acute and chronic applied to the characteristics of a disease or condition.

Synergist   A muscle that aids or assists the action of the prime mover but is not principally responsible for the movement.

Synovial Fluid   A thick, colourless fluid secreted by the membranes of the joint cavity.

Synovial Joint   A freely moving joint that has movement in one or more planes of action.

References

Apley, A. G. and Solomon, L.: 1997. Physical Examinations in Orthopaedics. Butterworth Heinemann, Oxford.

Armour, W. J.: 1983. The FA Guide to the Treatment and Rehabilitation of Sports Injuries. Butterworth Heinemann, Oxford.

Arnheim, D. D.: 1999. Dance Injuries: Their Prevention and Care. Princeton Book Co., USA.

Basur, et al.: 1992.

Blakey, P.: 1992. The Muscle Book. Bibliotek Books, Stafford.

Briggs, J.: 2000. Sports Therapy Course. Northern Institute of Massage.

Caldwell, E. A.: 1990. Sports Therapy Course. Northern Institute of Massage.

Cyriax, J.: 1974. Textbook of Orthopaedic Medicine. Bailliere Tindall, London.

Dornan, P. and Dunn, R.: 1987. Sporting Injuries. Butterworth Heinemann, Oxford.

Fairclough, J. et al.: 1992. Sports Injuries. Gower, London.

Grisogono, V.: 1984. Sports Injuries: A Self-help Guide. Murray, London.

Howse, J. and Hancock, S.: 1988. Dance Technique and Injury Prevention. A&C Black, London.

Hungerford, M.: 1993. Beyond Sports Medicine. Sports Massage Training Institute, USA.

King, R. H.: 1993. Performance Massage. Human Kinetics, USA.

Lachman, S.: 1988. Soft Tissue Injuries. Blackwell, Oxford.

Macnicol, M. F.: 1998. The Problem Knee.
Butterworth Heinemann, Oxford.

Minter, N.: 1999. To Strap or not to Strap – That is the Question.
Hockey Sport, March, 1999.

Peterson, J., and Renstrom, P.: 1986. Sports Injuries –
Their Prevention and Treatment. Martin Dunitz, London.

Sperryn, N.: 1983. Sport and Medicine.
Butterworth Heinemann, Oxford.

Spilken, T. L.: 1990. The Dancer's Foot Book.
Princeton Book Co., USA.

Vincent, M. D.: 1999. The Dancer's Book of Health.
Princeton Book Co., USA.

Index

Useful Addresses

Dance Books Limited
Old Bakery
4 Lenten Street
Alton
GU34 1HG
Tel: 01420 86138
www.dancebooks.co.uk

Mail order booksellers of dance related books,
and also publishers of *Dance Now*.

Merseyside Dance and Drama Centre
13–17 Camden Street
Liverpool
Tel: 0151 207 6197

Northern Institute of Massage
14–16 St. Mary's Place
Bury
BL8 4HZ
Tel: 0161 797 1800

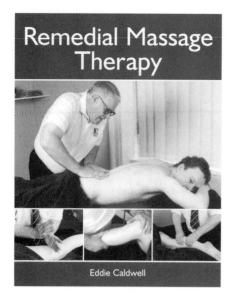

ISBN: 1 903333 02 4
Price: £15.00

Remedial massage has rocketed in popularity over the past five years. There are now more courses than ever before which offer the student the opportunity to learn this highly versatile technique which can be used on numerous conditions and in a variety of situations, from the confines of a treatment room to the sports field.

Fully illustrated with black and white photographs and line drawings, **REMEDIAL MASSAGE THERAPY** takes a comprehensive look at all aspects of remedial massage. Key areas covered include:

- The History of Massage
- Different Massage Techniques including Sports Massage
- Muscles and Joints
- Assessing and Treating the Patient
- Advertising the Practice
- A Fully Detailed Section Which Covers Treatment of Specific Areas of the Body
- Treating Children
- Origins, Insertions and Actions of Muscles

REMEDIAL MASSAGE THERAPY is full of useful, practical advice from one of the most experienced and respected practitioners in the UK, and will prove an extremely useful reference tool for any student or practitioner.

Eddie Caldwell, B.Ed. (Hons), L.C.S.P. (Phys), A.C.P., has been the Principal of the Northern Institute of Massage since 1995. Eddie qualified as a teacher of Physical Education in 1961 and gained further diplomas in Special Education at Manchester University, Sports Science at Salford College of Technology and Manipulative Therapy at the Northern Institute of Massage. The Northern Institute is accredited by the Open and Distance Learning Quality Council, and is the official training establishment for the London and Counties Society of Physiologists, established in 1919.